John Willingham's
World Champion
Bar-B-Q

John Willingham's

World Champion

Bar-B-Q

Over 150 Recipes and Tall Tales for Authentic, Braggin'
Rights, Real Southern Bar-B-Q and All the Fixin's

William Morrow and Company, Inc.
New York

It is the policy of William Morrow and Company, Inc., and its imprints and affiliates, recognizing the importance of preserving what has been written, to print the books we publish on acid-free paper, and we exert our best efforts to that end.

Willingham, John.
[Real Bar-B-Q]
John Willingham's World Champion Bar-B-Q: over 150 recipes and tall tales for
authentic, braggin' rights, real southern bar-b-q and all the fixin's.
        p.   cm.
        ISBN 0-688-13287-1
        1. Barbecue cookery.   I. Title.
        TX840.B3W54 1996
    641.5'784—dc20   95-47436
                CIP

Printed in the United States of America

            3   4   5   6   7   8   9   10

BOOK DESIGN BY CAROLINE CUNNINGHAM

I dedicate this book to the members of my family who contributed so greatly to my childhood basic training during the Great Depression and who continue to influence my life today. Much of their teachings are reflected throughout this book.

My grandmothers, Paralee Willingham and Effie Dorr, cooked on wood-burning ranges in Bevier, Missouri. They didn't mind my childish questions or my being constantly underfoot while they cooked for our clan. Oh, how those ladies could cook.

My mother, Vaunceil (little bit of heaven), always found the good in every situation and never complained even when I dirtied every pot, pan, and dish in our family kitchen. She always encouraged and cheered me on, regardless of whether I won or lost. She taught me to believe in my self-worth and that the cup was half full as opposed to half empty. If everyone had a mom like mine, what a wonderful world this world would be.

My father, Elmer Willingham, was a disciplinarian who taught me to play by the rules. He taught me how to clean and butcher the game we hunted. He invented an oil-fired floor furnace. He was my "you can do it, Sonny" coach. The word "can't" just didn't exist in his vocabulary.

My brother, Ever Ray Willingham, was a person who truly loved his fellow man. He was a master craftsman and he made my drawings and sketches come to life. He fabricated my first W'ham Turbo Cooker and the personality embodied in that cooker continues in our current designs.

And finally, last but certainly not least, there is my wife, Marge, and our three daughters, Kristi, Kara, and Karla, who made my marinade formula in a thirty-gallon garbage can while I convalesced several months following a major heart attack. They never gave up on me or the marinade formula. If they had given up, the seasonings, sauces, and mustard formulas would not exist today and this book would have never come to be.

Acknowledgments

If I could acknowledge everyone who had something to do with this book, my list would read like an MGM cast of thousands, reaching from Memphis to New York. Because space is limited, I want to express my thanks to the following:

My agent, Bill Adler, followed his instincts and brought me and William Morrow together.

Will Schwalbe, editor-in-chief, had the idea for this book and the courage to grant me the opportunity of a lifetime to share my recipes and to write about my beliefs, my recipes, cooking methods, and my love for the subject of Bar-B-Q, regardless of how you spell it.

Betty Lane, my secretary and friend, helped locate my scattered notes for the original manuscript. She transcribed my rambling thoughts and recipes from tapes I dictated as I traveled to and from Bar-B-Q contests and caterings.

Mary Goodbody, recipe writer extraordinaire, organized my rambling, original manuscript into a near finished product.

Doris Cooper, my editor, gently but firmly pushed me to complete my task on the book. She was the final filter and deserves much credit for the finished book.

Kim Yorio, my publicist, offered encouragement during the very nervous days of deadlines, when my confidence was a bit lacking.

I also owe thanks to the sponsors and members of Willingham's River City Roosters, my Bar-B-Q cooking team. The original team consisted of Gary and Sally Dodds, Bob Andrews, Lon and Karen Venable, Mark Pierce, and Mike Mannes. Over the years, 256 people have worn the Willingham's World Champion Bar-B-Q Team T-shirt.

I have come to know and respect thousands of friendly Bar-B-Q competitors over the years. They make Bar-B-Q cooking a great sport that crosses all racial, political, religious, and geographical boundaries.

The promoters, producers, sponsors, volunteers, and Bar-B-Q aficionados who attend the competitions and support this entertaining family sport bring the contests to life. They provide 'Quers an arena in which we can present our ideas, methods, cookers, and recipes during friendly competitions. It is a realm that provides a wholesome atmosphere where friends, family, and business associates can play.

And, finally, I want to acknowledge the most important people in the life of this book, the ultimate judges, the readers.

Contents

Introduction

What is barbecue? Let me begin by explaining what barbecue is *not*. It is not simply the act of cooking a burger or marinated chicken breast on the backyard grill. True barbecue aficionados do not call that kind of cooking "barbecuing." They may call it delicious, easy, relaxing—but not barbecue.

So what the heck is barbecue? It's two things both connected to each other but both very different by definition. First, technically speaking, barbecue is the method of cooking meat at a low temperature for a long time—thus the phrase "low and slow"—in a closed chamber, using indirect heat produced by hardwood logs, chips, chunks, pellets, or charcoal. Second, socially speaking, barbecue is when two or more people get together to cook meat in a cooker, on a grill, in a pit, or in a smoker, either by laying the meat out flat on a grill, hanging it on hooks from a stationary rod or revolving carousel. In short, barbecue is the centerpiece of the South's social events, be they political, religious, or organized by the Junior League or Jaycees. This is true regardless of how you spell it. (The University of Virginia claims there are at least twenty-six variant spellings! If you have a special way of spelling "bubba que," we'd shore like to hear from y'all. Donchano!)

During cooking, the meat absorbs the essence and flavor of the wood. It slowly renders all its fat and when it's done, it just about falls from the bone, is wonderfully moist, and tastes like nothing else you have ever tasted. It tastes like barbecue. The cooking process flavors and tenderizes the meat, which is not necessarily achieved by marinades, dry rubs, or sauces swabbed on the meat during cooking.

I am not saying marinades and dry rubs don't have their place in barbecue. Both flavor meat in delicious ways, and give the guy who is doing the cooking something to do. And sauces are among the most important features of a barbecue meal—but generally they are added just before the cooking is finished or at the time the barbecue is eaten. The true glory of real Southern barbecue is all in the cooking. Once you get the cooking down, you are well on your way to making great barbecue.

This book provides you with the tools for creating your own masterpieces so that you can fully enjoy barbecuing as a relaxing hobby or sport. As a sport, barbecuing can help alleviate some of the stress we all face.

Am I getting ahead of myself? How can barbecuing be a sport? I'm talking about barbecue competitions, which are common throughout much of the country. Organized competitions began in the South and parts of the Midwest and have spread from these regions. John Walker claims his Covington, Tennessee, BBQ Contest is the world's oldest organized contest, and it may well be. If you have never attended a barbecue contest, you really owe it to yourself to check out a few. Look in the *National BBQ News* and *KC Bull Sheet* for information. You may even become so inspired that you will organize a contest in your own hometown.

Whether your interest is to organize, attend, or compete in barbecue contests or just in turning out great ribs, rubs, or punchy sauces, this book will tell you things you haven't read before. You will understand what barbecue is all about and you'll be able to talk the language of 'cuers, who all share an infectious love for their craft. Think of this book as a road map permitting you to find answers to your questions and, more important, I think, inspiring you to find more answers on your own. When you finish it, you will know the difference between spareribs, back ribs, and baby back ribs, between a loin and a tenderloin. You'll know where brisket comes from and how to make the best sauces, marinades, and dry rubs. And I hope you will have developed a big-time enthusiasm for barbecue.

John Willingham's

World Champion
Bar-B-Q

1

Competition Is My Life

This may seem an odd title for a chapter in a book about cooking—but I mean this in the truest sense of the word. I have been a competitor all my life, always trying for my personal best and meeting life's challenges. And, of course, I always aim to win!

For some of us competition begins at birth with sibling rivalry and goes on as we compete for grades, places on the student council and sports teams, for scholarships, and eventually for success in the workplace. As parents we sometimes push and pull our kids, wanting them to get more from life than we have gotten. There are parents who believe that if their children can excel at a certain sport and turn pro, they will be on easy street. But even professional athletes arrive at a point in their lives when they are no longer able to compete at the same skill levels with younger competitors.

When physical strengths begin to wane, many of us are frustrated. After all, who is going to keep score as we spend our time reading, playing cards, bingo, and shuffleboard? This is where barbecue comes in. I believe with all my heart that this is the next great American sport—regardless of your age. I can compete in barbecue contests, where I maintain a certain level of interest and physical activity while meeting new people, discussing new ideas, and going head to head with other like-minded and skilled people. Memphis in May in Memphis, Tennessee, and the American Royal in Kansas City, Missouri, are the barbecue contests to which I am the most attached—and they are about as big as they get!

Long before I thought of competing in barbecue contests, I was a competitor. I played football in high school in my home state of Missouri (winning all-conference honors and all-state). When I got to college at the University of Missouri, I soon concentrated on baseball, eventually playing semi-pro ball and then signing with the St. Louis Cardinals. I had not finished college, but was so anxious to play ball and so excited that our college team had won the College World Series in 1953, that I "went for it." But before my baseball career got going, I signed up for the draft, hoping to serve in the Korean conflict. It was while pitching for a team in the Army that I broke my wrist. When I returned to the Cards organization, my weakened wrist left me useless as a pitcher, so I tried catching. As hard as I tried, I just couldn't keep from blinking during foul tips and pop fouls. A catcher is not worth a flip if he can't catch foul balls!

After leaving the world of professional sports, I went to work for a company that manufactured precast, prestressed concrete—and from then on devoted my working life to building. This eventually led me to Operation Breakthrough, a program run by the Department of Housing and Urban Development under the Nixon administration. It was during this time that I became interested in cooking. During the 1960s and 1970s, I traveled the country and the world, helping to construct buildings and consulting on major projects. But it all ended in 1980 when I had a car accident, followed a few months later by serious coronaries. I decided it was time to slow down and reevaluate my life. What did I truly love? Barbecue. Plain and simple.

Memphis in May

I have been competing in the Memphis in May World Championship Barbecue Cooking Contest since 1983. I am proud to say I have taken my fair share of first-place prizes at this competition as well as at other contests here and there. I won first place in ribs in 1983 and the same year was Overall Grand Champion. I did the same in 1984. And so it went. I have won first-place trophies at nearly all the major barbecue contests, including the American Royal barbecue contest in Kansas City, Missouri; National Rib Cook-Off in Cleveland, Ohio; and the American Royal Invitational in Kansas City. (For a list of my major awards, see page 227.)

Not only is the Memphis in May contest the world's largest—according to both the 1990 *Guinness Book of World Records* and every red-blooded barbecue expert—but it takes place at Tom Lee Park right in my hometown of Memphis, Tennessee. Let me tell you, it's an event I don't want to miss.

The first Memphis in May barbecue contest was in 1977. At that time it was held in a single day and there were only a handful of barbecuers—but they were a dedicated and talented handful. The contest has grown so that now it runs for three days and attracts competitors from all over the world. Generally, about 250 teams compete, and while every last one is crazy about barbecue, I'd say only about a third are hard-core, live-or-die-for-barbecue 'cuers. These folks go from competition to competition with their customized cookers hauled around in rigs the size of small moving vans to full-sized trailers pulled by cover-the-road Peterbilt tractors and even eighteen-wheelers!

Memphis in May begins on a Thursday and runs through Saturday evening at six o'clock, when the prizes are announced. Setup begins on Thursday for cookers and continues through Friday night so that the teams are ready for the judges on Saturday morning. There are blind tastings and on-site tastings. At both, the quality of the cooked meat is of paramount importance. Not much else really matters. Sure, it's important to present ribs, shoulder, or the whole hog (the only three official categories for competition) in an attractive way, just as it's important to have a spruced-up presentation tent, a team that looks clean, neat, and enthusiastic, and a team captain who sounds knowledgeable and is willing to spin a few yarns about his product. But when you come right down to it, the proof is in the meat.

Tom Lee Park begins at the foot of Beale Street and meanders along the bank of the Mississippi River in the shadow of the great Memphis Pyramid. During Memphis in May, a visible haze of incredibly aromatic smoke hangs over the park and envelops all of downtown Memphis. There's music and dancing, as well as the usual fast-food stands, to entertain and feed the more than 240,000 folks who come to enjoy the partylike festivities. Many competitors, such as my team, the River City Rooters, sometimes sell barbecue to the general public, but others do not. Who can blame those who don't? It's serious business to prepare meat for competition—why make life more complicated by serving food too?

Five Key Elements for Prize-Winning Barbecue

- **Appearance**—the meat should look attractive on the plate or in the "blind" judge container.
- **Aroma**—the meat must smell distinctively fragrant.
- **Taste**—at first bite there should be a mini explosion first in your mouth, then in your throat as your taste buds go ballistic. The "explosion" begins as a symphonic concert of flavors that becomes a full-blown orchestral crescendo with no specific flavor, herb, or spice singularly identifiable.
- **Texture**—the meat's texture should be chewable. We do not want it mushy, tough, or stringy.
- **Memory**—this is the quintessential part of the barbecue experience. The overall memory of the food tasted should stay with you.

The serious competitors at Memphis in May compete in fifteen to twenty competitions all year long, accumulating points to become a BBQ Team of the Year and thus qualify for the American Royal Invitational, the Jack Daniel's, and MIM. They pour money into their cookers and rigs and sometimes recoup it in prize money on the BBQ circuit, where top prizes reach $40,000—and will most likely reach $100,000 before too long. Some competitors sell the product (barbecue) or market sauces and marinades. Others have "day jobs" to fuel their barbecue passion.

In the old days, barbecue was cooked in a pit. Obviously, this is not a practical way to compete. You can't travel around the countryside digging pits and lighting fires in them. But you can build a cooker that cooks meat long and slow and exactly to your specifications—which is what makes perfect barbecue. The cookers may be large affairs, generally designed with an enclosed cooking chamber and a firebox, where hardwood—sometimes charcoal—smolders, producing even, slow heat, which cooks the meat (for more, see page 10). My past life as an engineer helped me design the first W'ham Turbo Cooker in which I hang the meat so that not a drop of fat hits the fire or firebox, which is completely separate from the cooking chamber. Not a single cinder touches the meat; there's hardly any smoke—only heat. This is clean cooking.

My First Cookers

My first competitive cooker was not as high-tech and efficient as the ones I build today—but it was a big black beauty with a red roof that enabled me to walk away with the championship the very first time I competed at Memphis in May. But let's begin at the beginning . . . more than a decade before that day.

In 1971 I accepted a political appointment during the Nixon Administration in Washington, D.C., with the Department of Housing and Urban Development under the Operation Breakthrough program. I moved to the nation's capital, leaving my family at home in Memphis, and took an apartment in a high-rise building. On the balcony was a small Weber kettle-style grill balanced on two wheels and a post. I cooked many meals on that contraption and faced the problems every outdoor "chef" does in terms of timing and irregularities with the weather. Still, the idea of cooking with fuel that I supplied (as opposed to the electric or gas company), and that was subject to the variables of outside temperatures and wind, intrigued me. In the middle of one night in 1971 I awoke and made sketches for a cooker that would have all the characteristics that currently are embodied in the cooker I now use—an efficient firebox and clean cooking chamber—and called W'ham Turbo Cooker WC-12BYVC.

The idea stayed with me for years but not until I was long back in Memphis did I act on the original sketches. Late in 1978 I was working with a company called Southern Fabricators, which was building about $250,000 worth of portable precast concrete molds for me for a building project (a luxury condominium called Paradise Manor) in the Cayman islands. And as consuming as that project was, I was still hell-bent on getting my cooker built. It became a personal crusade.

Having been frustrated by an experience with an industrial engineer who did not understand the sketches and specifications for my dream cooker, I asked Jim Cannon at Southern Fabricators to make the parts for the cooker. I sketched it on his blackboard early one morning and by the middle of the same afternoon, not only had he fabricated the parts and delivered them to my brother, Ever Ray, he and Ever, along with Dub Dodds, had assembled the parts and had a fire going in it by the time I arrived. We cooked some steaks right then and there, and then loaded the cooker into the back of a pickup truck and hauled it home—with the fire still burning in it! Three guys unloaded it in my backyard—along with a washtub of iced beer and soft drinks—and within a very short time, the neighbors arrived. We cooked ribs, steaks, and hot dogs, and the cooker just sat there and acted like it knew what it was doing. As my buddy Dean Osmundson commented, that cooker had its own personality.

During the next four years, with the help of my brother, Ever, and Dub, I made several improvements. In 1983, I went to my friends at Plant Maintenance and Service Corporation in Memphis with more sketches to build a cooker for competition—my first. By that time, I had decided to enter Memphis in May and needed the best cooker I could design. PMSC painted the cooker inside with orange primer, which refused to dry before the day I had to transport it to the competition site or risk being disqualified. I'll never forget how the more experienced 'cuers made fun of Gary Dodds and me as we eased the cooker into Tom Lee Park, both of us covered with smears and streaks of orange primer and black and red paint. They told us you had to "burn a cooker" for at least six months, or at least for fifty or sixty cooks, before it was seasoned enough to produce first-rate barbecue. "Hey, donchano?!" they laughed.

"Heck, man, you're never going to get anything cooked that tastes worth a hoot in that thing!" was the general message of their good-natured jeers. "Looks like an outhouse on wheels. When ya gonna pop the corn?"

But those same folks who teased us so unmercifully were cheering the loudest when the next day I walked off with First Place in Ribs and Overall Grand Champion. I have often wondered if anyone painted the inside of his cooker with orange primer the following year!

2

How to
Cook Barbecue

 We all know there are many types of cooking appliances called "barbecues" or, more accurately, "grills." If you want to make authentic barbecue, you need to buy or build a cooker that suits your needs. For small jobs, you can adapt a large kettle-style grill (such as a Weber) for barbecuing.

Grills come in all shapes and sizes—you probably have one in the backyard or on the patio. They are fine cooking apparatuses and are called for in many recipes in the book (see Chapter 6). Essentially, grills are grids placed over a direct source of heat. The heat is usually supplied by charcoal briquettes or, if it's a gas grill, by a gas-heated lava rock. Braziers, hibachis, and kettle grills fall into this category. There are also rotisserie grills, where the food is rotated directly above the heat. This is similar to spit cooking.

When I talk of barbecue I talk of cooking food in a cooker, or, as some folks call it, a smoker. I object to the term "smoker," because it implies that the food is smoked, which is far from the truth. Smoking is a time-honored way of preserving foods (remember the old-fashioned smokehouses on every farm?) but it is accomplished at lower temperatures than barbecuing and often in a piece of equipment called a smoker. Therefore, I use the term "cooker" to describe accurately what is, in fact, a facsimile of the traditional barbecue pit dug in the ground.

A cooker is constructed of a cooking chamber and a firebox. Food is cooked away from the fire by heat (not smoke) that passes over and around the food. When you think of barbecue, stop thinking of smoke. Smoke is nothing more than dirt, wafting into the air from burning wood. It comes to rest as ash. When the wood is properly burned at the right temperatures for barbecue, it does not smoke.

A number of commercial companies are marketing cookers and if you want to try your hand at backyard barbecuing, investing in one might be the best idea you ever had. For small cooking tasks, you can build a fire on one side of your kettle grill, and position a drip pan beneath the grid where the meat will sit away from the direct heat. With the lid on and the vents only partly open, you can "barbecue" a slab of ribs or a small brisket. You will have to monitor the temperature of the fire and add fuel as needed to keep the heat low and the smoke at a minimum.

If you are like me and enjoy tinkering and figuring things out for yourself, you may choose to build your own cooker. (Many do-it-yourselfers like to begin with a large metal drum. Make sure it has never contained any toxic substances.) I am not promising your cooker will win any beauty contests, but it will produce the best darn barbecue you have tasted outside the top BBQ restaurants and authentic dives in the South. This is because you design it to your own particular specifications. See page 232 for a diagram of the W'ham Turbo Cooker.

Deciding on the right cooker must be a personal choice. No one else can make it for you. You have to decide how dedicated you are to the task, what is available in your area, and about the cost. You also have to decide if you want to compete on a local, state, regional, or national level—or if you simply want to make good, *real* barbecue that will get your neighbors' tongues waggin' as they extol your culinary prowess. Because I cannot divine what types of cookers my readers will use, I cannot be absolutely precise in the recipes in Chapter 5, "Slow-Cooked Heaven." I have provided instructions as far as temperature ranges and approximate times. You are going to have to be the final judge when barbecuing the pork or beef of your choice.

Defining a Cooker

Generally speaking, a cooker is an apparatus that contains a firebox and a separate cooking chamber. The box may be below or beside the cooking chamber, but the idea is to coax the heat from the fire over, under, and around the food and then finally up and out a chimney. The food is never, ever placed directly over the heat—otherwise you would be grilling—but it is laid on racks or, as is the case with my cooker, hung from hooks. It stands to reason that heat moving away from the fuel and toward the food will be cooler than the heat in the firebox. This is desirable. Barbecue is supposed to cook low and slow.

I hang the meat in my cooker and the renderings drip from the meat into a water bath. The cooker is designed to hold a whole hog, slabs of spareribs, and large or small butts and shoulders.

In days gone bye barbecue was cooked in pits dug into the ground. The fire was built at one end and the meat was suspended over the pit. This served several functions. It eliminated the problems of wind and cold or hot drafts, and it muffled the aroma so that wild animals and rival tribes were not attracted to the cooking site. The smoke produced also acted as a natural insect repellent.

While man probably has been cooking meat this way since the days of living in caves, pit barbecue has a more modern history in my native South. This kind of cooking takes hours, and if a whole hog was being cooked, folks gathered the night before to dig the pit, dress the animal, and build the fire. Then the fun would begin, as the cooks (usually men) gathered around the pit to make sure the fire never went out or got too hot. They would sit up all night, swapping stories and weaving the elaborate yarns that are so much a part of the cultural richness and oral tradition of the South.

Later, when barbecue went commercial in the early days of the twentieth century, it was not always sensible to dig a pit in the back lot behind the café or restaurant. Concrete or cinder block pit cookers attached to the building, free-standing, or in an outbuilding, were built to perform the same functions. Many of the small town barbecue joints still rely on these block cookers for their barbecue. In large cities such as Atlanta, New York, and Boston, fire codes and space preclude cooking barbecue this way and so urban establishments rely on smaller metal cookers or bring the meat in from somewhere outside the city where it has been partially cooked. The cook then finishes it on the premises. Depending on the cook, this can be *very good* barbecue—but it ain't ever going to be *great* barbecue!

In Memphis, there are several good barbecue houses that talk a lot about their pits. They are similar in that they all are above-grade and similar in construction. They are built of cinder block and brick with fire liners and chimneys with metal doors that open and close to the inside of the restaurant or into an outbuilding. They have gridirons (or grids) that sit at various levels above the fire pit, which is on the bottom of the pit. These pits cook the food low and slow and far enough away from the heat to maintain the correct temperature for barbecuing.

When I think of Memphis barbecue, I think of Kay's, the Rendezvous, Neely's, the Pig 'n Whistle, Corky's, Tops BBQ, Coleman's BBQ, Leonard's and Lyon's Place, and Bozo's in Mason, Tennessee. And of course there are many more! All cook low and slow. Most use charcoal, some only wood, and a few use wood, charcoal, and gas.

Cookers

As I did, you can build your own cooker. (On page 232 is a diagram illustrating how my cooker looks.) I got a great deal of satisfaction from building my own—I was able to plan, revise, and tinker to my heart's content. And my pleasure in the perfect barbecue I was able to produce was all the sweeter because I had designed the cooker myself.

A large metal drum (fifty-five gallons is a good size) is a satisfactory place to start if you want to make your own cooker. Cut it in half lengthwise or horizontally, attach the top and bottom with hinges, and set an expanded metal grate over the bottom half to create a grill to hold the meat. The trick is to design the cooker so that the meat is not directly over the heat source. You can also barbecue in a kettle-style grill (such as a Weber) by building the wood or charcoal fire on one side of the kettle and setting the meat on the grid on the other side of the grill so that grease does not fall into the fire.

An increasing number of small companies are manufacturing cookers not much larger than a good-sized grill and that will do a yeoman's job in the backyard. The companies are located mostly in the South and Midwest, where distribution tends to be greater than in the rest of the country, but the cookers are turning up in hardware and home stores all around the country.

Fuel and Heat

You should use wood, although charcoal is acceptable, for authentic barbecue. Hardwood burns slowly and evenly enough to produce perfectly cooked barbecue, but for a novice, good-quality charcoal can't be beat. You cannot burn a soft, resinous wood such as pine and expect any sort of success.

Throughout much of the South, oak and hickory are the woods of choice. When you drive down a country road in Tennessee, Alabama, or Mississippi you can smell hickory wood burning. As the aroma gets stronger, you can be pretty sure you are nearing a barbecue stand. Put on the brakes, treat yourself to a plateful of real barbecue and glass of sweetened ice tea, and set a spell. You won't be sorry.

Hickory became the wood used by most Southern 'cuers because it grew in the region. There are more than fifteen varieties of hickory wood in the South—if you don't know the difference, you can ruin a cookin'. For the same reason, oak and mesquite are used in much of Texas. Down in Louisiana and along the Gulf Coast, you will find pecan wood smoldering in barbecue pits and cookers. Some folks like maple for hams and poultry, and others toss some apple or cherry wood on the fire when they are cooking poultry. (Out west, I hear, they use alder wood for smoking salmon—but it's a stretch to call that barbecue!)

If you don't have a stand of hardwood trees behind the house, you can buy wood in stores that sell outdoor-cooking supplies. You can also buy chunks of wood that work very well in small cookers. Be sure the wood is properly aged; green wood will behave exactly as it does in the fireplace: It will smoke and sputter and downright refuse to burn. And in a kettle grill, predried and then soaked wood chips added to the charcoal fire provide the food with a nice woodsy flavor.

Let me add that a new product has entered the market that I predict will replace charcoal in large part for grilling and indirect cooking in backyard kettle grills. Pellets made from the sawdust of hardwoods will render petroleum-based charcoal briquettes obsolete one day and impart just as delicious flavor to the foods as those cooked with high-quality charcoal, wood, or chips.

The Right Temperature

Temperature is crucial to barbecue. It must be between 185 and 250 degrees Fahrenheit. To maintain a fire as cool and constant as this demands diligence on your part. My cooker is designed with an internal temperature gauge that can be read from the outside so that we know when to add more wood. You may have to rely on trial and error at first, but eventually you will figure how much wood to add to keep the temperature constant. Don't forget that the outside temperature and the wind velocity will make a difference, too, in the amount of fuel necessary.

As well as I know my cooker, cooking times vary according to the weather conditions. Ambient temperature and wind velocity can alter the cooking temperature from ten to one hundred degrees! More important, the variables of the meat can make a huge difference. The cut, size, thickness, weight, and internal temperature each can affect the cooking time and the temperature requirements.

I side with most good barbecuers and rely mainly on internal temperature to determine when a piece of meat is done. No matter how many thermometers and other gimgaws we have rigged up to our cookers, we also depend on the old-fashioned way to tell when something is done. We still "stick it with a fork." Push the fork into the thickest part of the meat and if it goes in easily and comes out just as easily, the meat just about done. If you can turn the fork 90 degrees and then remove it, the meat is done. If you can turn the fork 180 degrees and remove it, the meat is pure gossamer. Enjoy it!

This chart explains temperature ranges for all kinds of cooking (in degrees Fahrenheit). Because most home cooks are familiar with roasting and broiling, these temperatures may put barbecuing into perspective:

```
       0°  TO  140°F  =  COLD SMOKING

    140°  TO  185°F  =  SMOKING

    185°  TO  250°F  =  BARBECUING

    250°  TO  350°F  =  ROASTING

    350°  TO  450°F  =  COOL GRILLING

    450°  TO  550°F  =  HOT GRILLING

    550°  TO  1,700°F  =  BROILING (HEAT SOURCE ABOVE THE FOOD)

    1,700°F  =  TEMPERATURE AT WHICH MOST COMMERCIAL STEAK

        HOUSES BROIL AND GRILL
```

Of course, until you develop a 'cuer's instincts, you might want to rely on an accurate thermometer for gauging when the meat is done. Commercially manufactured cookers come with thermometers, but if you make your own cooker, a portable candy thermometer is a good choice—it registers temperatures higher than does a meat thermometer designed for oven use (which registers only internal temperatures). Make sure it is sturdy and large enough to insert in the cooking chamber through a tube and still protrude enough so that you can read it. Or rig it so that you can remove it easily without having to open the cooker. Position the thermometer so that it is as far inside the cooking chamber as possible without actually touching the meat. In this case, you want to determine the temperature of the environment (not the meat).

Most cookers are designed so that you can control the heat with vents and dampers. Of course, moderating the amount of fuel is the best way to control the temperature. Until you get the hang of your own cooker, it's a good idea to check the thermometer every thirty to forty minutes and to count on adding fuel every hour or so. Remember, you have to keep the heat really low for real barbecue—below 225 degrees Fahrenheit is my favorite cooking temperature.

Other Equipment

When I compete in the American Royal Invitational in Kansas City, the organizers provide all of us with chicken, ribs, pork butts, briskets, and lamb for cooking. I take plenty of heavy-duty, sealable plastic freezer bags to use for marinating the chicken and storing meat. They are handy for storing leftovers, too. I also carry garbage bags for the ribs, which I double-bag to prevent marinade from leaking should a bone poke through the first bag.

You should also have heavy-duty and latex (or rubber) gloves, tongs, large forks, a complete set of knives and knife sharpener, plenty of paper towels, paper plates, and napkins. Coolers are especially important—to keep the meat cool, to store it during marinating, and for leftovers.

But the most important piece of equipment to have when you barbecue is a good sense of humor and the ability to roll with the punches, because if something can go wrong, it will!

> The person who knows how to do a job will always have a job. The person who knows why the job is being done will always be the boss.

3

Starters

Spicy Nuts · Quesadillas · Salsa Vegas · Liver Bitty Bites · Smokin' Fastball Wings · Grilled Hot Wings · Mushroom Munchies · Deviled Eggs · Pimiento Cheese Spread · Smoked Mullet · Grilled Shrimp with BBQ Sauce · Broiled "Bar-B-Q'd" Oysters · Herky Jerky Beef · Bar-B-Q'd Pork Pizza

Some folks might call these recipes "munchies" or even hors d'oeuvres. What they are are the food you serve right away when the guests walk in the door. They are "walking around" food you can eat from your hand or a napkin—grab a handful of Spicy Nuts, a few Grilled Shrimp, or a couple of Deviled Eggs. Southern hospitality demands that you offer everyone something to eat and drink right away. Whether you're entertaining a neighbor who stopped by unannounced or a large crowd at a barbecue picnic, no one should stand around hungry or thirsty! While beer goes down nicely with these, so do sweetened iced tea and cold soda.

Spicy Nuts

(thanks to Lady Karen Anderson)

Serves 4 to 6

 Spiced nuts are great by the handfuls.

2	tablespoons (¼ stick) butter, melted
2	teaspoons Mild Seasoning Mix (page 171) or W'ham Mild Seasoning
½	teaspoon garlic salt
½	teaspoon seasoned pepper or Lawry's hot-n-spicy seasoning

⅛	teaspoon ground cumin
⅛	teaspoon freshly ground black pepper
⅛	to ¼ teaspoon chili powder
1	pound slivered almonds or chopped walnuts

Preheat the oven to 375°F.

In a large bowl, combine the butter, seasoning mix, garlic salt, seasoned pepper, cumin, black pepper, and chili powder. Stir well.

Add the almonds and, using a wooden spoon or rubber spatula, stir until they are evenly coated. Bake the almonds for 15 minutes, stirring once or twice, until browned.

Variation: *Add ¼ teaspoon of cayenne and omit the seasoned pepper and cumin.*

You'll never have a "second" chance to make a "first" impression! So be sure that the impression you give is an honest one and something you can do repeatedly without special effort or deceit.

Quesadillas

(thanks to Steve Prentiss)

Serves 4

I suggest sharing these quesadillas as appetizers, but a whole one per person makes a tasty main course too.

4   tablespoons (½ stick) butter
½   pound fresh spinach, tough stems
      discarded, washed and dried
4   5-inch corn tortillas
5   ounces Smokehouse Dixie
      Chicken (page 53)
4   ounces shredded Cheddar cheese
      or Monterey Jack cheese, or a
      combination of both

2   scallions (both white and tender
      green parts), chopped
½   cup sour cream, for garnish
½   cup salsa, for garnish

In a large sauté pan, heat 2 tablespoons of the butter over medium-high heat. Sauté the spinach for 2 to 3 minutes until wilted. Set aside to cool slightly.

Melt the remaining 2 tablespoons of butter. Brush one side of a tortilla with butter and lay it, buttered side down, on a waxed paper–lined baking sheet. Sprinkle it with half of the spinach, chicken, cheese, and scallions. Lay another tortilla over the filling and brush its top with butter. Repeat with the remaining tortillas and filling.

Heat a griddle or large skillet over high heat until hot. Reduce the heat to medium-high. Using a wide spatula, carefully transfer the 2 quesadillas to the hot griddle and cook for 2 to 3 minutes until the bottoms are lightly browned. Turn the quesadillas over to cook for about 1 minute longer until browned.

Transfer the quesadillas to a cutting board. Using a serrated knife, cut each quesadilla into quarters. Serve with sour cream and salsa on the side.

Note: *You may replace the sautéed fresh spinach with ⅓ cup thawed and drained frozen leaf spinach. Squeeze the spinach to release the moisture; there is no need to sauté it in butter. Reduce the amount of butter to 2 tablespoons.*

Salsa Vegas

(thanks to Les Kincaid)

 Salsa is America's number one favorite condiment. Here's the best there is, in my opinion. Great texture, just enough spice, and fresh as can be.

3	medium tomatoes, finely chopped	1	tablespoon apple cider vinegar
5	to 6 green onions (both white and tender green parts), finely chopped	2	tablespoons Worcestershire sauce
		½	teaspoon garlic powder
½	cup finely chopped celery	1	teaspoon crushed dried oregano
1	4-ounce can green chiles, rinsed and chopped	3	to 4 dashes hot pepper sauce
2	tablespoons chopped cilantro	½	teaspoon freshly ground black pepper, or more to taste

In a medium-sized glass or ceramic bowl, combine all the ingredients. Toss gently, cover, and refrigerate for at least 1 hour.

Serve at cool room temperature with chips or as a topping for burgers.

The salsa will keep in a covered glass container for 2 to 3 days in the refrigerator.

Liver Bitty Bites

(thanks to Charles K. Bowen)

Serves 6 to 8

 Even "non-liver-lovers" like the taste and texture of these little grilled strips. They're meant to be eaten with your fingers—so don't stand on ceremony here!

2   cups Worcestershire sauce or All-Purpose Marinade (page 181) or W'ham Marinade

1   pound calves liver, cut into 6-inch-long and 1-inch-wide strips (approximately 24 pieces)

In a shallow glass or ceramic dish, pour the Worcestershire sauce over the liver strips. Cover with plastic wrap and marinate at room temperature for 30 minutes, or in the refrigerator for up to 2 hours.

Prepare the grill (or preheat the broiler). Ignite the coals and let them burn until covered with white ash.

Grill the strips for 2 to 3 minutes on each side until firm and cooked through. Serve directly from the grill.

Smokin' Fastball Wings

(thanks to Steve Uliss)

Serves 6

Although this recipe is based on Buffalo chicken wings (so named because they were "invented" in a bar in Buffalo, New York), these barbecued wings are better-flavored than any in the world! The blue cheese dressing and celery sticks are a tradition.

¼ cup All-Purpose Marinade (page 181) or W'ham Marinade

24 chicken wings

2 tablespoons Mild Seasoning Mix (page 171) or W'ham Mild Seasoning

2 tablespoons Cajun Seasoning Mix (page 172) or W'ham Cajun Hot Seasoning

¼ cup bottled blue cheese dressing, for serving

12 celery sticks, for serving

In a shallow glass or ceramic dish, pour the marinade over the chicken wings. Cover with plastic wrap and marinate at room temperature for 15 minutes, or in the refrigerator for up to 2 hours.

Start the cooker (pages 11–13) using hickory or apple wood and heat it to a temperature of 205°F.

Remove the wings from the marinade and shake them dry. Lay the wings on a waxed paper–lined baking sheet and sprinkle with half the seasoning mixes. Using your fingertips, rub the seasonings into the meat. Turn the wings over and sprinkle with the remaining seasonings and rub them into the meat.

Cook the wings in the cooker for 1½ hours.

Prepare the grill (or preheat the broiler). Ignite the coals and let them burn until covered with white ash.

Grill the wings for 4 to 5 minutes on each side until crispy. Serve with the dressing and celery sticks.

Grilled Hot Wings

(pure Willingham)

Serves 8 to 10; makes 48 pieces

When you're tossing the chicken wings with the seasonings, it's a good idea to wear a pair of rubber gloves—the seasoning can smart a little. I buy five-pound bags of chicken wings at shopping clubs and warehouse stores where they tend to package food in large quantities. These are great just off the grill and even better when dipped into a fiery sauce.

1 5-pound bag chicken wings, first and second joints only

1 cup Mild Seasoning Mix (page 171) or W'ham Mild Seasoning, or Cajun Seasoning Mix (page 172) or W'ham Cajun Hot Seasoning

1 recipe W'ham Hot Wings Sauce (page 186) or Dip 'em Hot Wings Sauce (page 187), for dipping

Disjoint the wing parts, discarding the flipper portion (which just gets in the way). Rinse, drain, then pat dry with paper towels.

Place a third of the wing parts in a large bowl and sprinkle them uniformly with a third of the seasoning mix. Using your hands, toss the wings and seasoning. Transfer the first batch to another large bowl or plastic garbage bag. Repeat with the remaining wings and seasoning mix, a third at a time. Combine the coated wings in one bowl or plastic bag. Cover, if using a bowl, and refrigerate for at least 1 hour and no longer than 4 hours.

Prepare the grill or preheat the broiler. Ignite the coals and let them burn until covered with white ash. Line a large roasting pan or shallow casserole with foil.

Remove the wings from the refrigerator about 20 minutes before grilling.

Grill the chicken wings in batches, about 4 inches from the coals or heat source, for 3 to 4 minutes a side until the juices run clear when the meat is pierced with a fork. When the wings are cooked, transfer them to the foil-lined pan. Cover loosely with foil to keep them warm while the remaining wings are grilled. If the air is especially cool, use a cloth towel to cover the wings. Serve with the sauce on the side for dipping.

Mushroom Munchies

(thanks to Paul Kirk)

Serves 6 to 8

 Use good-sized, well-shaped mushrooms for this easy appetizer. They're garlicky, with a hint of soy sauce and everyone loves them!

1½ pounds mushrooms
6 tablespoons (¾ stick) butter or margarine, softened
1 garlic clove, minced or pressed
3 tablespoons shredded Monterey Jack cheese

1 tablespoon dry white wine
1 teaspoon soy sauce
⅓ cup fine cracker crumbs, such as from saltines or water crackers

Preheat the broiler.

Trim the stems from the mushrooms and discard. Melt 2 tablespoons of the butter and brush it over the mushroom caps. Arrange the mushrooms, cavity side up, on a rimmed baking sheet.

Blend the remaining 4 tablespoons of butter with the garlic and cheese. When it is smooth, stir in the wine, soy sauce, and cracker crumbs and mix thoroughly.

Mound the filling evenly in the mushrooms, using your fingers to press it gently into the cavities.

Broil the mushrooms about 6 inches from the heat source for 3 to 4 minutes until the filling is lightly browned and bubbling.

> *Baking soda on a damp cloth will remove grime and grease from the glass on an oven door.*

Deviled Eggs

(thanks to Jim "Trim" Tabb)

Serves 6 to 8; makes 12 deviled eggs

What's a get-together without deviled eggs? When you add a pinch of the hot season-ing I designate as being "for big kids only," you'll be extra glad you thought of making these oldies but goodies.

6 large hard-boiled eggs	Drop of red wine vinegar
1 tablespoon sweet pickle relish	Pinch of sugar
¼ teaspoon prepared mustard	Paprika, for sprinkling
¼ teaspoon mayonnaise	12 capers
¼ teaspoon salt	Pinch of Hot Seasoning Mix
¼ teaspoon freshly ground black	(page 173) or W'ham Hot Stuff
pepper	Seasoning (optional)
¼ teaspoon dried fenugreek	

Peel the eggs and cut them in half horizontally. Scoop the yolks out and put them in a bowl. Set aside the scooped-out whites.

Add the relish, mustard, mayonnaise, salt, pepper, fenugreek, vinegar, and sugar to the yolks and mash with a fork until well mixed.

Carefully spoon the yolk mixture into the whites, mounding the filling. Top each egg with paprika and a caper.

For those with a burning desire, add a pinch of seasoning mix to each egg. This will light up your life.

Pimiento Cheese Spread

(pure Willingham)

Makes about 2 cups

A good smear of this rich cheese spread on crackers or slices of French bread whets the appetite. It's also great on celery sticks. And of course, it makes a filling sandwich spread too.

1 2-ounce jar pimientos	1 teaspoon Mild Seasoning Mix
2 cups grated Cheddar cheese	(page 171) or W'ham Mild
(about 8 ounces)	Seasoning
⅓ cup mayonnaise	Dash of Tabasco sauce
1 teaspoon prepared mustard	

Drain the pimientos and reserve the liquid in the jar. Coarsely chop the pimientos and put them in a food processor fitted with the plastic blade. Add the cheese, mayonnaise, mustard, seasoning mix, Tabasco sauce, and reserved pimiento liquid. Process until smooth.

Spread the mixture on crackers, bread, or celery.

Smoked Mullet

(thanks to Rodney S. Thompson)

Serves 4 to 6

Smoked fish is a genuine treat. I like to use Lawry's Seasoned Salt for this recipe, but any seasoned salt works fine—your choice. The fish is smoked at 250°F, which produces smoke rather than the lower heat required for barbecuing.

| 1- to 2-pound mullet | Store-bought seasoned salt |

Start the cooker (pages 11–13) and heat to a temperature of 250°F.

Fillet the mullet, leaving the scales and skin intact but removing the rib cage. Wash well under running water and pat dry with paper towels.

Lay the fillets on the smoking rack and sprinkle with the salt. Let them stand for 30 minutes.

Cook in the cooker for 20 minutes. Serve warm, at room temperature, or chilled, with crackers or bread.

Grilled Shrimp with BBQ Sauce

(thanks to Les Kincaid)

Serves 4 to 6

Shrimp boats ply the waters off the coasts of the southern Atlantic states and the Gulf of Mexico. Tennessee may be landlocked, but nonetheless here as throughout the South, shrimp are crowd pleasers.

It's always best to buy shrimp in the shell because they're apt to be fresher. Peel off the shells with your fingers and devein the shrimp by cutting out the black membrane running along their outside curve. This makes a great appetizer, but it's equally good as a main course for two. I like to use the hot stuff for the marinade, but you may prefer a milder sauce.

1½ pounds large unshelled shrimp (12 to 14 shrimp)	⅓ cup canola oil
2 cups Hot Bar-B-Q Sauce (page 157) or W'ham Hot Sauce	½ teaspoon salt
	⅓ cup freshly squeezed lemon juice

continued

Shell and devein the shrimp.

In a medium-sized glass or ceramic bowl, toss the shrimp with the barbecue sauce and oil. Cover and refrigerate for about 1 hour.

Prepare the grill or preheat the broiler. Ignite the coals and let them burn until covered with white ash.

Lift the shrimp from the marinade and thread 2 to 3 shrimp each on metal skewers, each 6 to 8 inches long. Grill for 2 to 3 minutes, turning several times and basting with the marinade, until opaque and cooked through. Sprinkle the shrimp with the salt and lemon juice and serve immediately.

Broiled "Bar-B-Q'd" Oysters

(pure Willingham)

Serves 3

 Oysters are a rare treat, and serving them with a little tangy barbecue sauce makes them a treat worth waiting for.

6 oysters in the shell (the kind of your choice)	2 tablespoons Hot Bar-B-Q Sauce (page 157) or W'ham Hot Sauce
6 1-inch squares pancetta (Italian bacon)	

Preheat the broiler.

Shuck the oysters, discarding the top shells. Set the oysters, still in the bottom shells, in a shallow roasting pan large enough to hold them snugly in a single layer.

Top each oyster with a square of pancetta and a teaspoon of the barbecue sauce.

Broil for 3 to 4 minutes until the oysters are heated through. Serve immediately.

Herky Jerky Beef

(thanks to Birgit Andes)

Serves 12 to 14

In the old days, cowboys and hunters preserved salted beef in the sunshine, letting it dry out so that they could carry it with them and chew on it when they felt hungry. I can't help but believe that jerky must have been akin to shoe leather. Not this version! It's tender and tasty. Liquid smoke is easy to find in supermarkets and specialty stores and really provides great flavor.

1	3-pound beef brisket, sliced into ⅛-inch-thick strips	1	to 2 tablespoons garlic powder
		1	teaspoon liquid smoke
1	cup soy sauce		

Put the brisket in a large glass or ceramic bowl and add the soy sauce, garlic powder, and liquid smoke. Stir to mix and turn the meat to coat it with the marinade. Cover and refrigerate for 8 hours or overnight.

Preheat the oven to 200°F.

Lay the strips of brisket on 1 or 2 baking sheets. Bake for 6 hours with the oven door propped open about 1 inch. Serve warm or at room temperature.

The cooked brisket will keep for 2 to 3 days stored in a tightly covered container and refrigerated.

Bar-B-Q'd Pork Pizza

(thanks to Steve Prentiss)

Serves 4

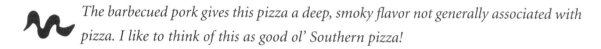 *The barbecued pork gives this pizza a deep, smoky flavor not generally associated with pizza. I like to think of this as good ol' Southern pizza!*

1 10-inch flour tortilla	¼ cup freshly grated Parmesan cheese
¼ cup Sweet Bar-B-Q Sauce (page 158) or W'ham Sweet 'n Sassy Sauce	Chopped red bell peppers, for garnish (optional)
4 ounces Bar-B-Q'd Pork Shoulder (page 42)	Chopped onions or green onions, for garnish (optional)
½ cup shredded mozzarella cheese (about 2 ounces)	Crumbled potato chips, for garnish (optional)

Preheat the oven to 350°F.

Lay the tortilla on an ungreased baking sheet. Bake for 4 to 5 minutes until crisp, turning once during baking. Remove the tortilla but do not turn off the oven.

Heat the barbecue sauce in a small saucepan set over medium heat until warm.

Spread the pork in an even layer in a shallow microwave-safe dish. Microwave on high (100 percent) power for about 1 minute, or until hot.

Brush a thin coat of barbecue sauce over the tortilla. Spread the pork evenly over the sauce and sprinkle the cheeses over the pork. Bake for about 2 minutes until the cheeses melt.

Cut into 8 wedges and serve, topped with peppers, onions or green onions, and crumbled potato chips, if desired.

4

Biscuits, Rolls, and Breads

Southern-Style Biscuits · No-Knead Refrigerator Rolls · Angel
Biscuits · Popovers · Overnight Potato Rolls · Rainbow Island
Corn Bread · Hush Dem Puppies · Corn Fritters

Southerners, who over the centuries have honed their baking abilities to enviable heights, lay claim to making the best homemade breads anywhere—and we eat bread with nearly every meal. We also have a fondness, not keenly shared in other parts of the country, for hot breads. Give a Southerner a piping hot biscuit or piece of corn bread, or a hush puppy so hot it still sizzles, and you have a happy person. There's a well known cliché in these parts that you should butter two biscuits before you eat one, so that the butter can melt on both.

In the old days, only the rich plantation owners and successful merchants could afford finely milled white flour—the rest of the Southern population had to rely on coarsely ground whole-grain flour and cornmeal. Such privilege gave rise to the mystique of tender biscuits made with white flour. They were served only in the "best" homes and soon became a regional treat and specialty and the cooks who produced them were much sought after. From there it was a short journey into Southern culinary heritage. Today, Southern biscuits represent some of the best baking of the region.

Rolls and corn breads, which often are served as hot breads, have long been popular too. Although not much corn is grown in the South, local cooks discovered ways of using cornmeal daily, resulting in mouth-watering recipes for corn bread, fritters, and hush puppies, as well as spoon breads and griddle cakes.

Southern-Style Biscuits

(pure Willingham)

Makes 8 biscuits

Nothing tops a biscuit baked by a good Southern baker. Because the wheat grown in the region is soft wheat, the flour milled from it produces especially tender biscuits. It's no secret that flaky, tender, melt-in-your-mouth biscuits are as much a result of soft flour as they are of the wonderful cooks who bake them (well … almost as much!). Down South we also are known to rely on self-rising flour, which works well in this recipe. And these are extra moist and tender because they are made with sour cream. Baking them in muffin pans is handy.

16 tablespoons (2 sticks) lightly salted butter, at room temperature, cut into pieces

2 cups sour cream
2 cups self-rising flour

Preheat the oven to 425°F.

In a mixing bowl, combine the butter, sour cream, and flour. Mix with a spoon until the dough holds together. It will be a wet dough.

Drop the dough into 8 ungreased muffin tin cups, filling each about two thirds full. Bake for about 15 minutes, or until lightly browned. Turn the biscuits out of the pans and serve hot.

No-Knead Refrigerator Rolls

(thanks to Charlotte Helton Patterson)

Makes 20 to 24 rolls

The dough for these rolls keeps in the refrigerator for a week, so you can pinch off only what you need for baking.

1	scant tablespoon (1 package) active dry yeast	2	teaspoons salt
½	cup sugar	1	large egg
2	cups warm water	¼	cup solid vegetable shortening
		6½	to 7 cups all-purpose flour

In a large bowl, dissolve the yeast and 1 teaspoon of the sugar in the warm water. Let the mixture sit for about 5 minutes until it bubbles and foams.

Add the remaining sugar, salt, egg, and shortening. Stir until well mixed.

Begin adding the flour, a cup at a time, and mix until the dough holds together in a cohesive mass and is not sticky. Shape the dough into a ball. Cover and refrigerate for at least 4 hours.

Pinch off the desired amount of dough. Store the remaining dough in the refrigerator for up to 1 week. Shape the dough into balls and put each ball in a nonstick muffin tin cup or on a nonstick baking sheet. Cover and set aside in a warm area of the kitchen for about 1 hour to rise until doubled in volume.

Preheat the oven to 450°F.

Bake for 20 to 25 minutes until golden brown.

Angel Biscuits

(thanks to Jo Grisham)

Makes 30 biscuits

Angel biscuits are traditional throughout the steep mountains of the central South. The dough keeps for up to a week and you can bake one or more biscuits as your appetite moves you. Why the name? Because the biscuits are light and heavenly. Be sure to knead the chilled dough for several minutes to activate the cold yeast.

5½	teaspoons (2 packages) active dry yeast	1	tablespoon baking powder
½	cup warm water	½	teaspoon salt
5	cups all-purpose flour	2	tablespoons sugar
1	teaspoon baking soda	1	cup solid vegetable shortening
		2	cups buttermilk

In a bowl, dissolve the yeast in the warm water. Let the mixture sit for about 5 minutes until it bubbles and foams.

In a large mixing bowl, sift together the flour, baking soda, baking powder, salt, and sugar. Cut in the shortening until the mixture resembles coarse crumbs. Add the buttermilk and the yeast mixture. Stir with a wooden spoon until the flour is moistened and holds together in a cohesive mass.

Shape the dough into a ball and put it in an airtight container. Refrigerate for at least 4 hours and up to 1 week.

Preheat the oven to 400°F. Grease a baking sheet.

Pinch off as much dough as you need and knead it on a lightly floured surface for several minutes. Store the remaining dough in the refrigerator. Roll or pat it out to a thickness of about ½ inch. Using a 2-inch biscuit cutter or upturned glass, stamp out the biscuits. Lay the biscuits on the baking sheet. Bake for 12 to 15 minutes until golden brown.

Note: *You can replace the buttermilk with soured milk. To sour milk, stir a tablespoon of apple cider vinegar or lemon juice into each cup of milk.*

Popovers

(thanks to Alice Parker)

Makes 8 popovers

 Popovers balloon up with air during baking, which makes them look puffy. You have to eat them when they're ready—don't wait on ceremony with these!

1	cup sifted all-purpose flour	2	large eggs, lightly beaten
1	teaspoon salt	2	teaspoon vegetable oil
1	cup milk		

Preheat the oven to 450°F. Generously grease 8 popover or muffin tin cups.

In the mixing bowl of an electric mixer, combine the flour and salt. Add the milk, eggs, and oil and, with the mixer set on medium-high, beat until smooth. Let the batter sit for a few minutes.

Put the well-greased popover tin in the hot oven for about 5 minutes until good and hot. Using oven mitts, take it from the oven and pour enough batter into each cup to fill it about halfway. Bake for 20 minutes. Lower the oven temperature to 350°F and bake for an additional 20 minutes. Do not open the oven door during baking! Serve the popovers right away.

> Friends need love too—especially when you think they do not deserve it.

Overnight Potato Rolls

(thanks to Mary Lee Marcom)

Makes about 36 rolls

These rolls are commonplace throughout the South (they used to be called icebox rolls). This dough can sit in the refrigerator until you're ready to bake the rolls. And what a great way to use up leftover mashed potatoes—but be sure the potatoes are not salted or seasoned with garlic or something else that might make for odd-tasting rolls.

1 scant tablespoon (1 package) active dry yeast	⅔ cup solid vegetable shortening
⅔ cup plus 1 teaspoon sugar	1 cup cooked and cooled mashed potatoes
1½ cups warm water	2 large eggs, lightly beaten
1¼ teaspoons salt	About 7 cups all-purpose flour

In a large mixing bowl, dissolve the yeast and the 1 teaspoon of sugar in the warm water. Let the mixture sit for about 5 minutes until it bubbles and foams.

Add the ⅔ cup of sugar, salt, shortening, potatoes, and eggs, stirring until well blended. Add 2 cups of the flour and stir until smooth. Gradually add as much of the remaining flour as possible, working it into the dough with a stout wooden spoon or your hands. Depending on the humidity of the day, you may not need all the flour.

Turn the dough out onto a lightly floured surface and knead it 10 to 15 times. Put the dough in a lightly oiled ceramic bowl, cover it loosely with a kitchen towel or waxed paper, and refrigerate for at least 12 hours or for as long as 24 hours.

Preheat the oven to 400°F.

Pinch off chunks of dough about 2 inches round and roll them out on a lightly floured surface to the shape of a dinner roll. Set the rolls on ungreased baking sheets, cover with a kitchen towel, and let them rise in a warm, draft-free part of the kitchen for about 2 hours until almost doubled in bulk.

Bake the rolls for 10 to 13 minutes, or until golden brown. Serve 'em hot.

Rainbow Island Corn Bread

(thanks to Lib Sossaman)

Serves 6 to 8

The sour cream and onion, as well as the cream-style corn, give this corn bread a delectable texture.

1¾ cups yellow or white stone-ground cornmeal	1 cup sour cream
¾ cup vegetable oil	½ cup cream-style corn
2 large eggs, lightly beaten	1 small onion, chopped
	2 tablespoons bacon grease or butter

Preheat the oven to 375°F.

In a bowl, mix together the cornmeal, oil, and eggs.

Put the sour cream, corn, and onion in a blender or food processor and mix until smooth. Stir into the cornmeal mixture.

Put the bacon grease in a 10-inch cast-iron skillet or 9-inch square baking pan. Heat the skillet in the oven for 3 to 4 minutes, or until the grease is hot (or the butter melts) and the skillet is very hot. Remove the skillet from the oven and set on top of the stove.

Immediately pour the batter into the hot skillet. Bake for 35 to 40 minutes until a toothpick inserted in the center comes out clean and the corn bread pulls away from the sides of the skillet. Serve hot or warm.

Note: *For a glazed bread crust, brush the top of the loaf with a mixture of one egg yolk and two tablespoons of water before baking.*

Hush Dem Puppies

(pure Willingham)

Makes 20 to 24 hush pups

I like these hush pups hot from the frying oil, but some folks prefer them served at room temperature alongside a big glass of ice-cold buttermilk. The first hush puppies were simply fried bread that was tossed to the dogs in a fishing or hunting party as a way to keep the critters quiet in the evening. Mine are seasoned and flavored with onions and peppers and definitely not meant to be thrown to the dogs! Everyone seems to like these served with fish. Anyway you eat them is fine with me—just try them!

4	cups yellow cornmeal	4	large eggs, lightly beaten
1	teaspoon Mild Seasoning Mix (page 171) or W'ham Mild Seasoning	1	teaspoon garlic powder
		¾	cup vegetable oil, plus more for deep-frying
½	cup all-purpose flour	1¼	cups water
⅓	cup sugar	1	red bell pepper, chopped
1	medium onion, finely diced		(optional)

In a large bowl, combine the cornmeal, seasoning mix, flour, and sugar. Stir in the onion, eggs, garlic powder, and the ¾ cup of oil. Mix well and then stir in the water. Add the red pepper, if desired.

Heat the oil in a deep-fat fryer or deep skillet to 350°F. Scoop the dough by tablespoonfuls and drop them into the hot oil. Fry each hush pup for 3 to 4 minutes until golden brown. Remove them with a slotted spoon and drain on paper towels. Repeat until all the dough is cooked. Serve them hot.

Corn Fritters

(thanks to Rodney S. Thompson)

Makes 8 to 10

Corn fritters are great with grilled meats and poultry—but if you want to serve them for breakfast or as dessert, dust them with confectioners' sugar when they're hot.

2	cups all-purpose flour	4	tablespoons (½ stick) butter,
1	tablespoon baking powder		melted and cooled
1	teaspoon salt	1	cup fresh or defrosted frozen corn
4	tablespoons sugar		kernels
2	large eggs, lightly beaten		Confectioners' sugar, for dusting
1	cup milk		(optional)

In a large bowl, combine the flour, baking powder, salt, and sugar. Stir in the eggs, milk, and butter. Mix well and then stir in the corn.

Heat the oil in a deep-fat fryer or deep skillet to 350°F. Scoop the dough by tablespoonfuls and drop them into the hot oil. Fry each fritter for 3 to 4 minutes until golden brown. Remove them with a slotted spoon and drain on paper towels. Repeat until all the dough is cooked. Serve them hot, dusted with confectioners' sugar, if desired.

5

Slow-Cooked Heaven: Real Barbecue

~

Bar-B-Q'd Pork Shoulder · Willingham's World-Champion Ribs ·
Jailbird Ribs and Sauce · Bar-B-Q'd Country Sausage · Smokehouse
Dixie Chicken · World-Champion Brisket ·
The Baron of Beef Brisket · Shredded Roast of Beef · Screamin'
Mean Oven-Roasted Beef Barbecue · South Carolina–Style Pork ·
Jubilation Plantation BBQ

~ The recipes in this chapter are the center, the very *heart,* of the book. Here you will find my tried-and-true recipes for real barbecue, along with some recipes shared with me by dear friends. You will also find a few recipes that do not require a barbecue cooker, but that you cook on the stove, in the oven, or on the grill. I included them here because these particular recipes require slow cooking—very, very slow cooking to give the flavors time to mingle and develop, just as they do in real barbecue. All fit under the heading "slow-cooked heaven."

Barbecue is cooked low and slow in heat supplied by hardwood or good charcoal and maintained between 185 and 250 degrees Fahrenheit. I like to maintain the temperature inside my cooker at 225 degrees Fahrenheit or lower to ensure the cooking is uniform and gradual—nice and slow. The slow cooking impregnates the meat with the essence of the wood and when combined with the flavors of the added spices (in rubs and marinades) and the meat's own juices, this spells barbecue.

The meat is not set directly over the heat source, as it is in grilling (during grilling the renderings fall onto the coals). Instead, the heat passes over, under, and around the meat, enveloping it in a low-temperature cocoon. After hours of cooking in this gentle, moist heat, the meat just about falls from the bone, is delicious and moist, and tastes like *only* barbecue can taste. It does not taste like anything else! Remember, it's the heat, not smoke, that cooks the meat. Low and slow heat. Smoke is not desirable.

Some barbecue houses cook directly over the coals or wood on multilevel grates and grills positioned far enough away from the heat to maintain a low temperature. Some use gas alone for heat, and others use gas to assist the wood or charcoal fire. Pure barbecue aficionados have trouble with the use of natural gas or liquid propane. I understand the problem, but frankly, the first three hours of cooking are the most crucial for using wood, charcoal, or wood pellets. After that time, the meat has released its own juices and formed a new "skin," effectively sealing out the aromatics produced by the heat source.

Before it's cooked, the meat is usually cleaned, trimmed, and rubbed with a dry mixture of spices, called a dry rub or seasoning mix, and then allowed to sit a while in a cool place. This gives the juices in the meat the opportunity to rise to the surface and mix with the seasonings so that in effect the meat "marinates" in its own juices.

In Memphis, we cook a lot of pork (although I find myself putting beef brisket in the cooker fairly often) and are inclined to stay with ribs and pork shoulder when barbecuing. Memphis in May is the only barbecue contest in the country that proclaims pork as the only meat for barbecue. I have included recipes for barbecued pork sausage, chicken, brisket, and roast beef, as well as recipes for porks ribs and pork shoulder. And, by the way, my recipes for ribs, shoulder, and brisket are based on award winners.

If you don't believe you can,
You won't.
If you always wonder if you should,
You will never know if you could.
And if you never ever try,
You will forever wonder why
What could have been but never was
Is because you didn't try.

I wrote this poem in memory of my father, Elmer Lawrence Willingham (1907–1969), who was my first and most enthusiastic baseball coach. He used to remind me before I pitched a game that on any given day, the weakest can beat the strongest—even if the strongest is the best.

It also reminds me of my football coach at the University of Missouri (Columbia, Missouri), the great Don Farot who passed away in October 1995. He was a leader, teacher, dreamer, disciplinarian, and, most of all, our friend and shining example. I remember when I was slightly injured during spring football in 1951 and his saying, "Spit on it, you won't remember it in a year from now." He was right. What he was saying was that if something minor interferes with your concentration and ability to compete up to your skill level, you should treat that interference as something inoffensive and not worthy of your attention. These principles apply in barbecue contests too. The better prepared, mentally and practically, the better you will do.

Bar-B-Q'd Pork Shoulder

(pure Willingham)

Serves 12 to 14

A fully cooked fifteen- to sixteen-pound pork shoulder yields about six to seven pounds of pure died-and-gone-to-heaven goodness. Use the pulled meat for barbecue sandwiches or serve it alongside Sweet 'n' Sassy Beans (page 112), coleslaw, or potato salad. Great anytime you want barbecue—weekend gatherings, big parties, or any good time.

1 15-pound pork shoulder	5 to 6 tablespoons Mild Seasoning Mix (page 171) or W'ham Mild Seasoning, plus more for sprinkling

Using a sharp knife, trim the skin and fat from the pork shoulder, leaving a 3-inch "sock" of skin and fat around the shank. Check for and remove any lymph nodes (clearly protruding small sacks) that are sometimes on the inside and back side of the shoulder, about two thirds up from the hock.

Lay the shoulder on a work surface and liberally sprinkle all over with the seasoning mix. Massage the mix into the meat, rubbing firmly to assure that the spice mixture penetrates the exposed muscle. Put the meat in a large pan, cover, and refrigerate for at least 2 to 3 hours and up to 24 hours to give the seasoning time to penetrate and develop its flavors. (The longer the better.) Let the meat return to room temperature before cooking to let most of the internal cold escape.

Start the cooker (pages 11–13). Cook the shoulder at 210° to 225°F for approximately

14 hours, or until it reaches an internal temperature of 185°F. You can also tell if the shoulder is done if you stick a fork into the meat and it easily rotates 360° and you can remove it with little resistance.

Shut down the cooker.

Set the pork shoulder on a work surface and let the meat cool to about 150°F. Using your fingers (you might want to wear latex gloves), pull the meat from the bones. Chop, chunk, or shred the meat and put it into a large bowl.

Sprinkle with seasoning mix and toss to coat well. Serve the meat right away. Or, put the still warm meat into heavy-duty self-sealing plastic bags, squeezing out as much air as possible before sealing the bags, or in several layers of plastic wrap, and refrigerate until ready to serve. Serve at room temperature or reheated in the microwave.

When storing meat in a self-sealing plastic bag, put the meat in the bag and then lay it on the countertop, flat side down. Zip it closed, leaving an inch to an inch and a half open. Press the contents of the bag so that they are a uniform thickness (one and a half to two inches) and then slide the zip seal closed. Stack the flattened bags in the refrigerator or cooler. The uniform thickness ensures that the meat will heat evenly.

Willingham's World-Champion Ribs

(pure Willingham)

Serves 4

This recipe has been good to me over the years, whether I'm in the backyard or cooking in competition. I've made ribs this way on television and on the barbecue circuit. First and foremost and without exception, the recipe will work equally well for any slab of pork, beef, or lamb ribs, regardless of the style, cut, or weight of the individual slab. (For more on ribs, see page 48.) Spareribs, which I call for in the recipe, are sold in slabs of thirteen ribs (bones) and should weigh in at about three and a half pounds.

When swabbing the ribs with the vinegar bath, I recommend you wear latex gloves. It's important to douse the meat with the liquid—it opens its pores and removes any residual bone dust too. The open pores permit the spices to penetrate the meat. During marinating—which can be accomplished in a covered pan or a sealed plastic bag—the pores close. After the ribs marinate in their own juices for ten to twelve hours, they look wet and tacky. During cooking, they go from looking wet to appearing dull and dry and then, when just about done, to looking dark, juicy, and glossy.

2   slabs spareribs (6 to 7 pounds)
½   cup apple cider vinegar mixed
     with ½ cup water, or 1 cup All-
     Purpose Marinade (page 181) or
     W'ham Marinade

6 to 7 tablespoons Mild Seasoning Mix
     (page 171) or W'ham Mild
     Seasoning

Lay the ribs in a nonreactive pan and brush on both sides with the vinegar water mixture. Sprinkle with seasoning mix and rub it in with your fingertips, massaging it into the meat. Cover and refrigerate for at least 12 hours.

Start the cooker (pages 11–13), allowing it to reach a temperature of 250°F. Put the slabs in the cooker. (If the cooker is fitted with a rotisserie or carousel, attach the slabs to the apparatus.) Cook for 4½ to 5½ hours, turning the meat every 15 minutes (unless it is attached to a rotating apparatus). The ribs are done when the internal temperature of the meat reaches 180°F, when the ribs are flexible, when the meat is fork-tender, and when the ends of the bone extend about ⅜ inch below the meat.

To serve, cut the slabs into individual bones or three-, four-, or six-rib racks. Serve immediately with or without your favorite sauce.

Note: *To store the ribs once they are cooked, let them cool to room temperature and wrap them in plastic wrap and hold at room temperature until ready to serve. Alternatively, hold the wrapped ribs in an insulated box for 2 to 3 hours, or refrigerate for a day or two. You can also freeze the ribs for up to a month.*

To reheat, puncture the plastic wrap and reheat them in a microwave for 2 to 3 minutes at high (100 percent) power, or, remove them from the plastic and heat them in a 300°F oven for about 20 minutes until hot.

A slab of ribs is a whole slab of thirteen ribs (bones)—the way God made it! A rack, on the other hand, can be anywhere from two to twelve ribs (bones), depending on how the chef, cook, or butcher chooses to offer it.

Jailbird Ribs and Sauce

(thanks to Lewis Fineberg)

Serves 4

Some foods are to die for (like these ribs!). Lewis always felt going to jail would be worse than dying. Rest easy, my friend. We all miss you. Pork ribs (either spareribs or meatier country-style ribs) are great when first marinated in this gingery brown sugar-based sauce. But try it with beef ribs too. (For more on ribs, see page 48.)

1½ cups packed dark brown sugar
1 cup light corn syrup
1 cup white wine
1 tablespoon olive oil
1 to 2 tablespoons honey
1½ teaspoons Mild Seasoning Mix
   (page 171) or W'ham Mild
   Seasoning

1 teaspoon hot pepper seasoning or
   Lawry's hot-n-spicy seasoning
½ teaspoon ground ginger
½ teaspoon dry mustard
4 pounds pork spareribs

In a saucepan, combine the brown sugar and corn syrup and cook over medium-high heat, stirring, until the sugar melts. Remove from the heat and add the wine and olive oil. Add honey to taste and stir well.

Add the seasoning mix, hot pepper seasoning, ginger, and mustard. Stir to mix. Cover and refrigerate for 24 hours.

Put the ribs in a shallow glass or ceramic dish and add the sauce. Cover and refrigerate for 8 hours or overnight.

Start the cooker (see pages 11–13). Cook the ribs at 225°F for 4½ hours until fork-tender. Serve immediately.

Note: *You may choose to bake the ribs in a 350°F oven for 1½ hours and finish on the grill. Reserve the sauce and brush it over the ribs at the end of baking. Grill or broil the brushed ribs for 8 to 10 minutes until browned.*

I like to cook at 225°F until the desired internal temperature is reached. Then, I shut the dampers, turn off the heat supply (or remove the heat source), and allow the thermal inertia of the meat's internal heat to continue to render and homogenize the flavors of the meat. When the internal temperature in the cooker drops to 150°F, I remove and wrap the meat. At that time, its internal temperature is still in the neighborhood of 170°F.

Pork

Whole pork loin: from the shoulder roasts to the ham and can weigh from ten to twelve pounds. It includes the loin back ribs, the pork loin, the tenderloin, and the pork chops. The loin, which is situated at the top of the hog, is considered the prime meat. In the old days during hog kill'n time, the plantation owners got the entire loin to eat, hence the expression "eatin' high on the hog" meaning eating well.

Pork loin: sometimes called a Canadian loin, runs along the top and for the length of the loin. Available with the bone in or boned. Generally weighs five to seven pounds, although if it's from a sausage sow, it can weigh up to nine pounds.

Pork tenderloin: from the underside and rear of the loin with the most tender meat. Weighs about one pound.

Boston butt: a shoulder roast also called a loin roast with a good amount of lean meat, which comes from a portion of the shoulder. Usually weighs six to eight pounds. By the way, they have never heard of Boston butt in the city of Boston—but you can buy it everywhere else.

continued

Country ribs: meaty ribs cut extra heavy from the blade end of the pork loin with no fewer than three bones/rack of ribs and no more than six bones/rack of ribs. I like to tie two six-bone racks together into a crown rack, submerge the crown in marinade for about two hours, and grill it over a medium-hot fire until the internal temperature of the meat reaches 125°F.

Loin back ribs: generally weigh from one and a half to two and a half pounds, however they can weigh as much as four and a half to five pounds (if they are from a sausage sow).

Baby back ribs: loin ribs from the back area of a young hog, containing at least eleven to thirteen ribs, depending on the butchering process. Usually weigh one pound, plus or minus one or two ounces. If the slab weighs more than eighteen ounces, it is not baby back ribs. Larger, heavier loin back ribs often are sold as "baby back ribs" by restaurateurs and other purveyors who either don't know the difference—or don't care.

Spareribs: from the lower part and sides of the chest just inside the bacon. These ribs house the lung cavity. The back side has a sinew membrane that contains the tallow oils from the spareribs. Spareribs have thirteen ribs (bones), and the tastiest meat in the hog lays between these ribs.

The most popular sparerib slab is what is commonly called a three and a half down, which means it weighs between three and three and a half pounds, has thirteen ribs and a 1½-inch skirt of meat on the sinew side about eight inches long (which I always remove). It has a portion of the breast plate, sometimes called the brisket plate, that primarily is hard cartilage at the upper end, and the tip (which looks and tastes like bacon) is reinforced with some more small, round, flexible cartilage appendages called feather bones. Folks in Memphis call these rib tips.

St. Louis spareribs: similar to other spareribs, but trimmed so that the breast plate and the feather bones along with the skirt from the back sinew side of the slab are removed. Usually weigh two pounds or less. I prefer St. Louis–style spareribs to loin back ribs for competition and overall cooking, believing the spares have more flavor than the loin ribs. I also believe spareribs were the first to be barbecued on plantations in the Old South. I say, if it ain't broke, don't fix it!

Pork shoulder: —consists of the shank, foreleg, and blade bone of the shoulder and contains both the picnic roast and shoulder roast (also called Boston butt). (Don't count on buying a shoulder in Memphis during the Memphis in May barbecue contest—can't do it! They're all being used in the competition.) Can weigh fifteen to twenty pounds.

Ham: —located at the rear of the hog and consists of the hind leg (hock, leg bone, and hip socket). The ham has the best meat-to-bone ratio and can weigh up to twenty-five pounds. The best for barbecuing weigh eighteen or nineteen pounds. Ask the butcher to remove the hocks, which are great seasoned and smoked and served with beans.

Meat (beef and pork) is considered barbecued when all the fat is rendered or when the internal temperature in the thickest parts reaches 180° to 185°F. Of course, the meat has to be cooked on a wood, charcoal, or wood pellet fire at temperatures between 185° and 250°F.

Beef

Rib roast (prime rib of beef):   from the rib section of the forequarter with the best, tenderest meat, weighing from twelve to fifteen pounds.

Round (rump) roast: from the top end of the hindquarter and usually rolled if the bones are removed and weighing about fourteen pounds.

Beef brisket: section of meat under the chuck, just above the forelegs. Good brisket is fatty—not dry. Weighs from six to sixteen pounds (depending on the size of the beef).

Short ribs: cut from the ends of the rib roast with layers of lean meat and fat between flat rib bones and have no more than five ribs. Weigh one and a half to three pounds.

Bar-B-Q'd Country Sausage

(pure Willingham)

Makes about 5 pounds;
about twenty 4-inch links

This sausage is about as good as it gets. If your meat grinder has a stuffing funnel, filling the casings is easy. Otherwise, use a hand funnel (see the Notes). It will take a little longer, but it's definitely worth the time! Buy the casings at a butcher shop.

3½ yards hog sausage casings

5 pounds coarsely ground pork shoulder

3 tablespoons salt

2 tablespoons freshly ground black pepper

2 tablespoons Mild Seasoning Mix (page 171) or W'ham Mild Seasoning

2 tablespoons ground sage

Put the casings in a large bowl and add enough cold water to cover by several inches. Let the casings soak for about 1 hour.

In a large shallow bowl or on a work surface, spread the meat out into a thin layer. Sprinkle with the salt, pepper, seasoning mix, and sage. Using your hands, mix well. Make sure the seasonings are evenly distributed.

Attach the stuffing funnel to the meat grinder and moisten it so that the casing will slide over the end easily. Push a little ground meat through the grinder so that it protrudes from the tip of the funnel. Slide the casing over the funnel, gathering it over the funnel so the entire casing is on the funnel. Hold the casing with one hand and begin feeding meat into the funnel. Fill the casings so that the sausage is about 2½ inches in diameter. Coil the sausage below the grinder so there is no pull on the casing.

Using twine, tie the casing into sausages every 4 inches for 4-inch sausages. Secure the ends of the casing with twine.

Start the cooker (pages 11–13) and let it reach a temperature of 200°F. Cook the sausages for approximately 8 hours, or until they reach an internal temperature of 160°F. Shut down the cooker. Serve warm.

For storage, cool to room temperature and then refrigerate for several days or freeze for up to 1 month.

Notes: *You may use a hand funnel to stuff the sausage. Slip the casing over the end of the funnel and proceed as described above. You may, if you choose, form the meat into patties rather than stuffing it into casings.*

Instead of barbecuing the sausage, fry the links in a frying pan over high heat for 3 to 4 minutes, or until cooked through.

I am convinced that minimum smoke provides me with the maximum assurance of a clean cook and the maximum release of aromatic essences from the wood into the cooking chamber. Therefore, as little smoke as possible means the best in terms of consistency, taste, and appearance. Too much smoke usually overpowers the meat and can leave a bitter taste.

Smoke is simply unburned particles of fuel (ash) that rise on a heat column. In the absence of light, there is no such thing as smoke, only ash. You can't see smoke in the dark. You can't smell smoke. What you smell is the essence of the fuel being consumed. So the next time someone says "I smell smoke," ask him what kind of smoke? Is it rubber tires? A bakery? An oil refinery? Or, perhaps, if you're lucky, it's a Bar-B-Q pit!

Smokehouse Dixie Chicken

(pure Willingham)

Serves 4 to 6

Chicken is not barbecued as often as other meats are—more commonly found in the cooker is pork or beef. But sometimes only tender, moist barbecue chicken will do. I assure you: This recipe is the best there is for barbecue chicken—better than all the rest.

2	2½-pound fryer chickens, trimmed and split	4	tablespoons Mild Seasoning Mix (page 171) or W'ham Mild Seasoning

Lightly rub each chicken half with 3 tablespoons of the seasoning mix, rubbing more into the bony side. Cover and refrigerate for at least 5 hours but no longer than 12 hours.

Start the cooker (pages 11–13), using hardwood. Cook the chicken at 210°F for 4 to 4½ hours, or until the thigh joint wiggles freely and the juices run clear.

Remove the chicken and sprinkle with the remaining 1 tablespoon seasoning mix. Shut down the cooker. Let the chicken rest for 15 minutes, loosely covered with foil, before serving.

Barbecue chicken is done when it is pierced and the juices run clear and when the meat pulls easily away from the bone. It's also done if the bone extends through the meat. If you like to rely on internal temperature tests, it's done when the temperature of the meat reaches 160° to 170°F. Remember, an old chicken takes longer to cook than a young one, and because it's a little tough, lean toward the higher internal temperatures.

World-Champion Brisket

(pure Willingham)

Serves 10 to 12

This recipe is for serious cookers only. The procedure is time-consuming, no argument there, but if you follow the recipe exactly, you will finish in the top 10 percent in any brisket competition—unless the other guy uses the same recipe! In that case, presentation will be the winning factor because people eat with their eyes first. Taking the time to prepare this brisket proves the adage that anything worth doing is worth doing right. Remember to establish good, steady heat inside the cooker. A cold brisket is a lot like a stubborn jackass, sometimes you have to hit el burro in the head with a two-by-four to get his attention. A brisket is the same about giving up its cold until it is overpowered by the initial and sustained heat that causes the pores to open, allowing the cold to escape rapidly. The most important thing to do after cooking and resting is to slice the meat across the grain into pieces about ¼ inch thick.

1 6- to 9-pound brisket with deckle	¾ cup Mild Seasoning Mix (page 171) or W'ham Mild Seasoning
½ cup All-Purpose Marinade (page 181) or W'ham Marinade	½ cup packed dark brown sugar
½ cup beer, cola, or club soda	

> *Don't be alarmed if there is a pink rim around the outside of the meat when you slice it. This is called a "smoke ring" and is supposed to be there when meat is properly barbecued.*

Stiff-back boning knife, sharpened   Meat thermometer

1   roll 16-inch-wide plastic wrap   Long-blade carving knife, sharpened

1   roll 18-inch-wide aluminum foil

Remove all the fat and sinew from the brisket, leaving ¼ inch of fat extending from the top of the brisket point. Cutting at a right angle to the grain, trim the corner off the brisket point. This will serve as a guide later when it is time to slice the brisket. This will also be important should you decide the direction to cut prior to pulling the brisket.

Rub the meat all over with the marinade and set aside, covered, for 20 minutes in a cool place.

In a bowl, combine the beer, seasoning mix, and brown sugar. Rub the meat all over with the mixture, massaging it in with your fingertips. Cover and refrigerate for at least 12 hours and preferably for 24 hours.

Start the cooker (pages 11–13), allowing it to reach a temperature of 250°F. Let the cooker remain at that temperature for 30 minutes to establish and ensure a uniform thermal inertia in the cooking tower or chamber. A brisket resists giving up its massive cold, so the fire must have a strong supply of basic heat to overpower and then to draw the cold from the meat. Once the dominance of the fire is established, the brisket will become a willing part of the cooking process.

Cook for 8 to 10 hours, maintaining a temperature of 210°F. The brisket is done when the temperature reaches 180° to 185°F internally or when a fork slides easily in and out of the meat. Remove and allow the brisket to rest for about 10 minutes. Wrap tightly with foil and put in the cooler part of the cooking chamber where the temperature is approximately 150°F. Let it rest until you are ready to serve it, or for about 1 hour. Serve it, sliced across the grain, basted with any accumulated juices.

Note: *The brisket can rest in an insulated cooler that has been filled with very hot water, drained, and dried. Cover the cooler with the brisket inside.*

The Baron
of Beef Brisket

(thanks to Paul Kirk)

Serves 10 to 12

Brisket is arguably the worst piece of meat God created on a cow. But when properly trimmed and rubbed with salt and pepper or seasoning mix, and then cooked low and slow over oak and hickory if barbecuing, or, as here, over a charcoal grill for 8 to 10 hours, it's indescribably tender and tasty. Nothing like it. In this recipe, the brisket is cooked in a kettle-style or other covered grill. You will have to baste it now and again and will have to add more coals to the fire to keep it smoldering.

1   9-pound brisket, trimmed
    (see the Note)
1   cup prepared mustard

5 to 6 tablespoons Mild Seasoning Mix
    (page 171) or W'ham Mild
    Seasoning
2 to 3 cups apple juice

Using a pastry brush, brush the fatty side of the brisket and down the sides with the mustard. Sprinkle with the seasoning mix. Turn the meat over and repeat on the lean side.

Prepare the grill. Ignite the coals and let them burn until covered with white ash. Pile the coals on one side of the grill. Set an aluminum foil pan in the empty space next to the coals. The pan should be as large as the brisket. Pour 2 to 3 inches of water into the pan.

Position the brisket over the pan, cover the grill, and cook for 8 to 10 hours. Make sure the grill cover is well vented. Baste the brisket with the apple juice after 4 hours. Baste it again after 2 hours and then again after another hour. (In other words, baste it every "half time"—halfway between the current time and the end of cooking.)

Add more coals to the fire and water to the pan as needed to keep the environment hot (190° to 220°F) and smoky.

The brisket is done when a fork slides easily in and out of the meat. Let the brisket rest for about 10 minutes before slicing it across the grain into thin slices.

Note: *For best results, buy a brisket in Cryovac (plastic packing bag). Wash and pat it dry with a paper towel. Trim the fat on the fatty (back) side so that it is ¼ to ⅛ inch thick (enough fat to hold moisture in the brisket during cooking). On the lean (top) side is a large pocket of fat; resist the temptation to dig this fat out. Instead, trim it so that it is even with the angle of the brisket (which will be between 30° and 60°). There is another pocket of fat on the side of the meat that should also be trimmed—but again, don't clean out all the fat.*

Many of my Texas friends wrap heavy cuts of meat in foil when the meat is done. They then set the puckets in an area of the cooker where the temperature is 140° to 155°F and let the flavors steep while the meat slowly cools to a temperature where it can be sliced without falling apart.

You always want to wrap meats while they are still hot! Wrapping hot meat at 140°F plus seals in the juices. By the same token, you are protecting the meat from any foreign airborne bacteria while it cools or is transferred to the refrigerator or freezer.

Shredded Roast of Beef

(pure Willingham)

Serves 10 to 12

For this recipe, the beef is cooked with a mixture of soy sauce and cola. (Yes! cola—although not diet soda. Why bother?) These liquids commingle deliciously with the juices rendered from the meat during cooking for a fantastic au jus. *Shredded beef makes a great sandwich or served alongside cold salads.*

1 6- to 8-pound round (rump) roast of beef	1½ cups cola, such as Dr Pepper, Coca-Cola, Pepsi, or Royal Crown
6 to 8 tablespoons Mild Seasoning Mix (page 171) or W'ham Mild Seasoning, plus more for sprinkling	¾ cup soy sauce

Start the cooker (pages 11–13) and heat it to a temperature of 225°F. Or preheat the oven to 225°F.

Rub the meat all over with the seasoning mix, massaging it into the meat with your fingertips.

Put the meat in a large Dutch oven and add the cola and soy sauce. Do not cover. Set in the cooker or the oven.

Cook for about 3 hours, basting every 15 minutes or so with the pan juices. Cover the Dutch oven with its lid or with foil and continue to cook until the beef's internal temperature reaches 185°F, or a fork stuck into the meat easily rotates 360° and can be pulled out with little resistance. Shut down the cooker.

Set the Dutch oven on a work surface and keep it covered. Let the roast cool in the juices until its internal temperature is about 155°F. With the roast still in the pot, cut the meat across the grain into 2½-inch-wide pieces.

Hold each piece of meat with tongs against the work surface. Using a salad fork or large tablespoon, shred the beef, drawing the tines or edge of the spoon across the grain of the meat. Put the shredded meat into a large bowl.

Sprinkle the shredded beef with enough seasoning mix, to cover with a light dusting. Skim the fat from the pan juices and then pour ½ cup of the juices over the meat. Discard the remaining juice. Toss to mix well. Serve the meat right away or put the meat in heavy-duty self-sealing plastic bags. Add the juices in the bottom of the bowl to the bags with the meat. Squeeze out as much air as possible before sealing the bags and refrigerate until ready to serve. Serve at room temperature or reheated in the microwave.

In my judgment, Gary Jacobs had more to do with bringing barbecue to the next dimension (professionalism) than any other single person in the country—or, for that matter, the world. Gary began the national rib cook-off in Cleveland, Ohio, in the early 1980s and was the promoter of the event until 1991. What a memorable contribution!

Screamin' Mean Oven-Roasted Beef Barbecue

(thanks to Les Kincaid)

Serves 6 to 8

Here's a can't-be-beat beef barbecue that cooks in the oven.

1	cup beef broth	1	tablespoon kosher salt
3	cups ketchup	1	teaspoon liquid smoke
½	cup cider vinegar		(see the Note)
¼	cup Worcestershire sauce	1	garlic clove, minced
¼	cup packed dark brown sugar	1	4½- to 6-pound chuck roast

In a large saucepan, combine the broth, ketchup, vinegar, Worcestershire sauce, brown sugar, salt, liquid smoke, and garlic. Bring to a simmer over medium-high heat and cook for about 30 minutes until blended. Remove from the heat and set aside to cool to room temperature.

Put the roast in a glass or ceramic dish and pour the cooled marinade over the meat. Cover and refrigerate for 2 hours, turning once or twice.

Preheat the oven to 325°F.

Lift the meat from the marinade, wipe off the excess, and set the meat in a roasting pan. (Reserve the marinade.) Cover and roast for 3 hours. Turn the meat once or twice and baste frequently with pan juices.

Remove the cover and brush with the reserved marinade. Continue roasting for about 30 minutes until the meat is fork-tender and reaches the preferred degree of doneness. Lift the meat from the pan and set aside for 15 minutes.

Pour the remaining marinade into a small saucepan and heat until boiling over high heat. Slice the meat very thinly and serve with the sauce.

Note: *Liquid smoke is readily available in supermarkets.*

South Carolina–Style Pork

(thanks to Les Kincaid)

Serves 12 to 14

In South Carolina they like their pork slow-cooked with a vinegary sauce, a custom throughout the eastern Carolinas. You'll like it too. This isn't traditional barbecue because the meat is cooked on a grill—but it's cooked low and slow nonetheless!

1   5- to 8-pound pork butt or 12- to
    18-pound pork shoulder, trimmed

2   cups South Carolina BBQ Sauce
    (page 169)

Prepare a charcoal or wood grill. Ignite the coals and let them burn until covered with white ash.

Put the meat on the grill about 5 inches from the coals. Sear it for about 2 minutes on both sides. Using a basting brush, baste the meat generously with the sauce. Cover the grill with the lid and cook for 15 minutes.

Baste again and continue cooking, basting every 15 minutes for a total of 1½ hours, or until the internal temperature is 185°F and the meat is done and starts to fall from the bone. Add more coals or wood as necessary to maintain a steady, moderate heat.

Transfer the pork to a cutting board and let it rest for 10 to 15 minutes before cutting it into bite-size pieces.

Heat any remaining sauce in a small saucepan just until boiling. Remove from the heat and let cool until tepid. Serve with the pork.

How you prepare the meat you're going to cook is critical. Begin by trimming it and then rub it with a dry rub, or, if you prefer, submerge it in a marinade. How long you let the meat sit and absorb the flavors before cooking is equally important, as is the type of holding container and the temperature of the meat during holding.

Jubilation Plantation BBQ

(thanks to William Shelton Monroe)

Serves 10

 This is great served on fresh buns or French rolls; don't forget the coleslaw, baked beans, and ice-cold beer. This brisket is cooked on top of the stove.

Meat

4   pounds brisket, chuck roast, or pork shoulder, trimmed

2   garlic cloves, slivered

1   cup cola, such as Dr Pepper, Coca-Cola, or Royal Crown

Sauce

3   tablespoons vegetable oil

2   onions, finely chopped

⅓   cup cider vinegar

⅓   cup packed dark brown sugar

1   cup ketchup

½   cup chili sauce

4   tablespoons Worcestershire sauce

½   tablespoon cayenne pepper

3   tablespoons spicy brown mustard

2   tablespoons kosher salt

2   garlic cloves, minced

Freshly ground black pepper to taste

Start the cooker (pages 11–13) and let it reach a temperature of 250°F.

To prepare the meat, using a small, sharp knife, make small incisions in the side of the meat and insert the garlic slivers in them, continuing until all the slivers are used.

Put the meat into a Dutch oven or large pot and add the cola. Cook, uncovered, for 2 hours. Reduce the heat to 200°F and cook for 4 hours, turning once after 2 hours. During the last hour of cooking, cover. The internal temperature should be 160°F.

Uncover and let the meat sit in the pot for about 45 minutes until its internal temperature reaches 150°F. Remove the garlic, wrap the meat in plastic, and refrigerate for at least 8 hours or overnight. Pour the cooking juices into a bowl, cover, and refrigerate.

About an hour before serving, remove the meat and juices from the refrigerator. Unwrap the meat and shred it, using your fingers or 2 forks to pull it apart. Cover and set aside at room temperature.

To prepare the sauce, in a large saucepan, heat the oil over medium-high heat. Add the onions and cook for 2 to 3 minutes until barely softened. Add the vinegar, brown sugar, ketchup, chili sauce, Worcestershire sauce, cayenne pepper, mustard, salt, garlic, and black pepper. Raise the heat and bring to a boil. Reduce the heat to a brisk simmer and add 1 cup of the cooking juices. Simmer for 15 to 20 minutes until slightly thickened. Add the meat, stir, and simmer gently until the mixture reaches 145°F. If necessary, add more cooking juices or water to keep the mixture moist. Serve immediately.

> The next time you get to the end of your rope,
>
> tie a knot and hang on—just hang on!
>
> —from my friend Jerry Hanriquez

6

Grills: Grilled Beef, Pork, Chicken, and Seafood

Holey Burgers · Grilled Beef Tenderloin · Bulgogi · Just-the-Way-You-Like-It Grilled Steak · Poodah's Beef Tender · Tenders in Wine Sauce · Grilled Pork Loin Roast · Grilled Pork Loin Chops · Down 'n Dixie Extra-Thick Grilled Pork Chops · Honey Mustard–Glazed Ribs · Hurry Yup BBQ Ribs · Pork Apple Kabobs · Grilled Veal Kabobs · Grilled Poor Man's Cordon Bleu · Grilled Chicken in-a-Pot · Hot Sauce–Marinated Chicken · Dancing Chicken · Marinated Chicken Breasts · Grilled Italian Herb Chicken Breasts · BBQ Swordfish · Herbed Shrimp with Basil · Grilled Shrimp with BBQ Sauce · South City Shrimp

Not all cuts of meat are meant to be cooked low and slow as some are for barbecue. And with very few exceptions, fresh water fish and seafood have no place in a barbecue cooker. But they are great grilled! So are hamburgers (I like mine with a hole in the middle, as you will see on page 66), steaks, tenderloins, chops, and ribs (which, of course, are also great barbecued).

This is where the familiar backyard apparatus, erroneously called a "barbecue" by so many people, comes into play. Build a charcoal fire (page 87), in a kettle grill, brazier, or hibachi and prepare delicious beef, pork, veal, chicken, or shrimp dishes in relatively short periods of time. Like a Southern barbecue social event, a backyard feast revolving around grilled food is a great way to bring folks together and have a grand old time.

Holey Burgers

(pure Willingham)

Serves 6

What is a Holey Burger? It's a burger with a hole right in the middle. What else? Years ago, I discovered that I had to overcook burgers to get the middle done the way my wife likes it (medium-rare). This meant sometimes cremating the edges of the dang things! Such abuse resulted in shrunken burgers that were practically burned around the edges and puffed up in the center. They looked pitiful and lonely in the middle of their buns. How to solve this? Poke a hole in the burger to allow the meat to cook evenly.

A rare burger may be the thing in big cities where chefs and fancy diners decry cooking anything beyond medium-rare, but I have found that about 60 percent of everybody who eats hamburgers likes them medium to well-done. And only about 10 percent actually likes them rare. Plus, no one likes shrinkage. The Holey Burger allows you to cook it to desired doneness without the usual shrinking.

Here's what happens when a regular hamburger cooks: As heat rises from its source, it kisses the bottom of the burger and then runs to the circumferencial edges of the meat. This overcooks the edges of the burger. The edges shrivel and shrink, and the center puffs up. This is why backyard cooks or chefs with a degree from culinary school are always flattening the sizzling burgers with a flat iron or stiff metal spatula. The hole in the burger eliminates this. Cook your next batch of burgers in half the time using this method for the juiciest burgers of all time. This works whether you grill, broil, bake, or barbecue (in a cooker) the burgers.

2   pounds lean ground beef
¼ to ½ cup chopped onions
        (optional)
3   tablespoons water
2   teaspoons salt
1   teaspoon lemon pepper

1   teaspoon light brown sugar
1   teaspoon freshly ground pepper
2 to 3 tablespoons soy sauce, All-
        Purpose Marinade (page 181), or
        W'ham Marinade

In a large bowl, mix the beef with the onions, if desired, until they are evenly distributed. Add the water, salt, lemon pepper, brown sugar, and black pepper and mix thoroughly.

You can make the burgers the size you want from four 8-ounce patties, six about 6-ounce patties, or eight 4-ounce patties. Flatten the patties to about ½ inch thick. Then, using an apple corer or your finger, poke a hole in the center of each patty. The hole should be about 1 inch in diameter for an 8-ounce patty, ¾ inch for a 6-ounce patty, and ½ inch for a 4-ounce patty.

Grill the burgers for 4 to 6 minutes, turning them once, for rare, 7 to 10 minutes for medium, and 11 to 12 minutes for medium-well. Just before they are done, brush them with soy sauce, turn the brushed side to the heat for about 30 seconds, and serve immediately.

Note: *To vary the seasonings, substitute 4 teaspoons Hot Seasoning Mix (page 173) or Cajun Seasoning Mix (page 172) or W'ham Hot Stuff Seasoning or W'ham Cajun Hot Seasoning for the salt, lemon pepper, brown sugar, and black pepper.*

Sometimes we must make a leap of faith based only on that inner voice that compels us to believe that something is fact when there is absolutely no proof to support that belief. Such as cold goes to heat. A dew point occurs when heat and cold meet. Less aroma is released from the piece of wood that is starved for atmosphere. A Holey Burger cooks more uniformly than a flat solid burger. Think about it: Where does the dew point occur on a glass of cold water? Outside! Where is the dew point on a cup of hot coffee? Well hey, it sure isn't on the outside, is it?

Grilled Beef Tenderloin

(thanks to John Marcom)

Serves 8 to 10

Until you've grilled tenderloin, you haven't tasted tenderloin! The flavor imparted to this tenderest of all cuts of beef by the grill is indescribable. For best results, let the tenderloin marinate for 24 hours. We served this at our daughter Karla's wedding reception. Wow! What a hit!

1	4- to 6-pound beef tenderloin, trimmed	3	tablespoons Mild Seasoning Mix (page 171) or W'ham Mild Seasoning
¼	cup All-Purpose Marinade (page 181) or W'ham Marinade		

Steak Butter

8	tablespoons (1 stick) unsalted butter or margarine, softened	1	tablespoon Mild Seasoning Mix (page 171) or W'ham Mild Seasoning

Lay the tenderloin in a glass or ceramic baking dish and pour the marinade over it, using your fingertips to rub it into the meat. Sprinkle the seasoning mix over the tenderloin and rub it in with your fingertips. Set aside to marinate at room temperature for about 20 minutes.

Make the steak butter by mixing the butter with the seasoning mixture.

Rub half the steak butter over the tenderloin. Cover the remaining butter and refrigerate. Put the tenderloin and any accumulated marinating juices in a plastic bag large enough to hold it. Press out as much air as possible and secure the top of the bag with a twist tie. Refrigerate for at least 12 hours and up to 24 hours.

Prepare the grill. Ignite the coals and let them burn until covered with white ash.

Meanwhile, remove the tenderloin from the plastic bag and let it come to room temperature. Grill for 25 to 30 minutes for rare, turning it in quarter turns every 4 minutes. Serve with the reserved half of the steak butter passed on the side.

Bulgogi (Korean-Style Barbecue Beef)

(pure Willingham)

Serves 6 to 8

 I modified this classic Korean recipe for grilled beef to my specifications. Can't be beat!

¾   cup water

½   cup soy sauce, All-Purpose Marinade (page 181), or W'ham Marinade

¼   cup chopped green onion (both white and tender green parts)

3 to 4 tablespoons sugar

2   teaspoons sesame oil

¾   teaspoon Mild Seasoning Mix (page 171) or W'ham Mild Seasoning, or 1 teaspoon salt and ½ teaspoon freshly ground black pepper

½   teaspoon chopped garlic

3   pounds sirloin, sliced across the grain into ¼-inch-thick slices

4   cups hot cooked rice

In a shallow glass or ceramic bowl, combine the water, soy sauce, green onion, sugar, sesame oil, seasoning mix, and garlic. Add the sirloin and stir gently to coat. Cover and refrigerate for at least 4 hours and for up to 12 hours.

Prepare the grill. Ignite the coals and let them burn until covered with white ash.

Lift the slices from the marinade and lay them on a fine-mesh grilling grid (a bulgogi) and grill for 4 to 6 minutes on each side. Serve immediately with the rice.

> **Things turn out best for people who make the best out of the way things turn out!**
>
> —Art Linkletter

Just-the-Way-You-Like-It Grilled Steak

(thanks to Dr. Dick Reynolds)

Serves 2

Cooking steaks on the grill is an American backyard tradition—expected and appreciated, with a dad in an oversized apron, playing outdoor chef. Preparing them this way, with plenty of seasoned butter sauce, guarantees tender, delicious results.

8-ounce sirloin or club steaks	2 tablespoons Mild Seasoning Mix (page 171) or W'ham Mild Seasoning

Sauce

8 tablespoons (1 stick) unsalted butter	2 tablespoons chopped parsley
½ cup beef broth	2 tablespoons sliced mushrooms (optional)

Rub the steaks on both sides with the seasoning mix. Lay the steaks in a shallow glass or ceramic dish.

To make the sauce, melt the butter in a small saucepan over medium heat. Add the broth, parsley, and mushrooms, if desired, and cook for 2 to 3 minutes, or until the mushrooms soften.

Pour the butter sauce over the steaks. Cover and refrigerate for at least 1 hour and up to 4 hours.

Prepare the grill. Ignite the coals and let them burn until covered with white ash.

Let the steaks come to cool room temperature. Lift them from the butter mixture and scrape off as much of the butter as possible. Grill the steaks for 3 minutes over the hottest part of the fire to sear. Turn and cook for 4 to 5 minutes longer for rare meat, and for 7 to 8 minutes longer for medium-rare.

continued

Meanwhile, transfer the butter mixture from the glass dish to a saucepan and heat gently until melted and warm. Serve the sauce with the grilled steaks.

Have you ever heard of "black and blue" meat? This is for folks who like meat—steaks and chops—rare or medium-rare. Rub marinade and dry rub (seasoning mix) into a good piece of meat that is about one and a quarter inches thick. Let the meat marinate for as long as you like (most steaks and tender chops need only twenty to thirty minutes). While the meat is marinating, let a cast-iron or other metal skillet (no non-stick surfaces) get red hot over a high flame. This can take a good ten to fifteen minutes or even a little longer. Drop the meat into the skillet and blacken each side. It takes only two to three minutes at the most to sear the sides of the meat. When you cut into the meat you will see that it is actually crimson red with tinges of blue. The outside is nice and crispy and very tasty. I confess, when I see blue meat I think "raw" and so I leave the meat in the pan for a little longer.

Poodah's Beef Tender

(thanks to Peter Pettit)

Serves 6 to 8

The marinade for this meat is truly what I would label "delightful." Wrapping the meat in foil for the last half of cooking captures the juices.

1	4½-pound beef tenderloin, trimmed	3	tablespoons olive oil
2	tablespoons sea salt	1	tablespoon chopped garlic
1	tablespoon freshly ground black pepper	1	tablespoon dry mustard
		1	tablespoon Worcestershire sauce
			Juice of 1 lemon

Rub the tenderloin with salt and pepper and lay the meat in a shallow glass or ceramic dish.

Whisk together the olive oil, garlic, mustard, Worcestershire sauce, and lemon juice. Pour the marinade over the meat and turn it several times until well coated. Cover and refrigerate for 1 to 2 hours.

Prepare the grill. Ignite the coals and let them burn until covered with white ash.

Lift the meat from the marinade and grill for 10 minutes on each side. Wrap the meat in foil and return it to the grill for 10 to 15 minutes. To test for doneness, insert a meat thermometer into the center of the thick end; it should read 110° to 120°F for rare meat. Let the tenderloin rest for about 10 minutes before slicing and serving.

Note: *If you prefer, transfer the foil-wrapped meat to a smoker and smoke it for about 45 minutes at 300°F.*

Tenders in Wine Sauce

(thanks to Sam Bomarito)

Serves 2

For nearly thirty years, I have enjoyed the exceptionally fine foods of the one and only Pete and Sam's Restaurant at 3883 Park Avenue, located just west of Getwell Road in Memphis, Tennessee. Pete and Sam's claim to fame? Just darn good food! My favorite entrée is Sam's Beef Tenders for Two and while this is not his exact recipe, I have come pretty close to duplicating it. At the restaurant, the dish is finished in a 500°F pizza oven. I have modified it for a backyard kettle grill, or kommado-type cooker.

1 cup dry red wine	1½ teaspoons Mild Seasoning Mix (page 171) or W'ham Mild Seasoning, or 1 teaspoon salt, 1 teaspoon freshly ground black pepper, and 1 teaspoon lemon pepper
1 4-ounce can mushrooms, drained	
¼ cup soy sauce	
4 tablespoons (½ stick) butter or margarine	
	2 6-ounce beef tenderloin fillets

Prepare the grill. Ignite the coals and let them burn until covered with white ash.

Meanwhile, combine the wine, mushrooms, soy sauce, butter, and seasoning mix in a shallow casserole dish.

Put the casserole dish on the grilling grid over the hot coals but to one side of the grill. Lay the fillets on the other side of the grill. Cover, making sure the vents in the lid are partially closed to maintain high heat (450° to 500°F).

Grill the meat for 5 minutes. Turn and cook for another 5 minutes. Remove the meat from the grill.

When the wine sauce is simmering, lay the fillets in the casserole. Spoon the sauce over the meat. With the lid off the grill, bring the sauce to a simmer again. Cook the fillets in the simmering sauce for an additional 4 minutes for rare meat, 8 minutes for medium-rare, and an additional 12 minutes for well-done. Serve the meat with the sauce spooned over the top.

Note: *Try this same method with pork loin cut about 1¼ inches thick, or with lamb chops. Great!*

The kommado cooker originated in China roughly four thousand years ago. It has recently been modified by Ed Fisher from Atlanta, Georgia, whose company is called The Big Green Egg. I have one of these grill/cookers and it is, in fact, shaped like an egg. My cooker also happens to be green! It works like a demon, cooking food really fast, which makes me excited about its future possibilities—particularly if we can add a pellet-fire system to it.

Grilled
Pork Loin Roast

(thanks to Darlene Ryan)

Serves 6

Grilling a whole roast is a challenge but one well worth it. For this, use a pork loin roast with the bone in—sometimes called a center loin pork roast or rib roast. It's a tender cut of meat and tastes great with a little seasoning.

1   to 1¼ cups All-Purpose Marinade (page 181) or W'ham Marinade

1   5-pound pork loin

3 to 4 tablespoons Mild Seasoning Mix (page 171) or W'ham Mild Seasoning

Prepare the grill. Ignite the coals and let them burn until covered with white ash.

Spread the marinade over the pork loin, covering it well on all sides. Sprinkle generously with the seasoning mix.

Insert a meat thermometer into the center of the pork loin, taking care not to insert it through fat. Set the pork loin on the grill, cover, and grill for about 1 hour. Make sure the lid is well vented during grilling, and add more coals as needed.

Remove the meat from the grill when the internal temperature reaches 170°F. Let the pork loin rest for about 5 minutes before slicing and serving.

Grilled
Pork Loin Chops

(thanks to Darlene Ryan)

Serves 2

~ *When marinating these chops, don't let them sit out for too long—only until their surface temperature reaches the temperature of the surrounding air. When she prepares
these beauties, Darlene's husband, Rex, is in charge of grilling and he insists on a well-oiled
grilling grid (the place where the meat sits). If the grilling grid is not nicely oiled, he says he'll get
oiled!*

2   tablespoons plus 2 teaspoons All-
    Purpose Marinade (page 181) or
    W'ham Marinade

4   boneless pork loin chops (about
    2½ pounds)

2   tablespoons plus 2 teaspoons
    Cajun Seasoning Mix (page 172)
    or W'ham Cajun Hot Seasoning

Prepare the grill. Ignite the coals and let them burn until covered with white ash. Oil the
grilling grid.

Spoon about 1 teaspoon of the marinade over one side of each chop and rub it in with your
fingertips. Turn the chops over and repeat. Set the chops aside for about 5 minutes.

Sprinkle about 1 teaspoon of the seasoning mix over one side of each chop and rub it in
with your fingertips. Turn the chops over and repeat. Set the chops aside in a glass or ceramic dish
to marinate at room temperature for no longer than 30 minutes.

Grill the chops for 6 to 7 minutes on each side until cooked through. Serve immediately.

Down 'n Dixie
Extra-Thick Grilled
Pork Chops

(pure Willingham)

Serves 4 to 6

Butchers call eight-ounce pork chops that are cut so that they are an inch and a quarter thick America's cut chops. Very few people can eat more than one. Soaking them first in salted water makes them more receptive to the flavors of the seasoning (sprinkle it liberally!) and the basting sauce (slather it on with gusto!). I always wear latex gloves when working in salt water to keep it from stinging.

6	8-ounce boneless pork chops, about 1¼ inches thick	½	cup Mild Seasoning Mix (page 171) or W'ham Mild Seasoning
2	tablespoons salt	1½	cups Mild Bar-B-Q Sauce (page 155) or Mild W'ham Sauce
2	cups water		

Rinse the chops and set them aside.

Stir the salt into the water until dissolved and pour the water into a shallow glass or ceramic dish large enough to hold the pork chops in a single layer.

Lay the chops in the water and let them soak for 4 to 5 minutes. Turn them over and let them soak for 4 to 5 minutes longer. Rinse the chops under cold running water and pat them dry with paper towels. Pour the water from the dish and wipe it dry.

Sprinkle both sides of the chops with the seasoning mix and rub it into the meat with your fingertips. Return the chops to the dish and let them marinate in their own juices for at least 30 minutes or as long as 2 hours. (If marinating them for longer than 30 minutes, cover with plastic wrap and refrigerate the chops.)

Prepare the grill. Ignite the coals and let them burn until covered with white ash. Oil the grilling grid.

Grill the chops about 4 inches from the coals. Cover the grill and let the chops cook for 5 minutes (the temperature of the grill should be about 350°F). Turn the chops, brush them with barbecue sauce, close the lid, and grill for 6 minutes. Test for doneness by cutting one chop open to see if the juices run clear. If they are not done, baste them again with sauce and grill them for 2 to 3 minutes longer until done.

Warm the remaining sauce in a saucepan over medium heat and serve it alongside the chops.

Definitely do not use lighter fluid when starting a fire. Lighter fluid, oil, coal oil, diesel oil, gasoline—any of these is a mistake, a big mistake! Any one will contaminate the cooker and will certainly contaminate the taste of what otherwise would be good food. Let the fire, your heat source, have plenty of atmosphere so that it smokes as little as possible. On the other hand, if you are using chips, such as cherry, hickory, oak, apple, or whatever, soak them for ten to fifteen minutes before you put them on the fire; their "smoke" is short-lived but the flavor they impart is long on taste. Soaking maximizes the aromatic release from the chips to the cooking chamber.

Honey Mustard–Glazed Ribs

(pure Willingham)

Serves 2

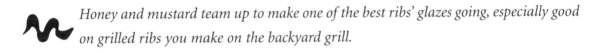

Honey and mustard team up to make one of the best ribs' glazes going, especially good on grilled ribs you make on the backyard grill.

2	tablespoons (¼ stick) butter	½	teaspoon salt
½	cup chopped onions	½	teaspoon grated orange peel
1	cup honey	2	tablespoons orange juice
⅓	cup white wine vinegar	4	pounds spareribs or pork loin
1	cup country-style Dijon mustard or Willingham's Old Phartz Mustard		

Heat the butter in a large saucepan over medium-high heat. Add the onions and cook for 5 to 7 minutes, stirring occasionally, until softened. Stir in the honey, vinegar, mustard, salt, orange peel, and orange juice. Continue cooking for 6 to 8 minutes until boiling.

Reduce the heat to medium low and cook for 8 to 10 minutes longer until the glaze thickens slightly and the flavors blend. Remove from the heat and measure out ½ cup of the glaze. Set aside the remaining glaze (there will be approximately 1½ cups).

Meanwhile, prepare the grill. Ignite the coals and let them burn until covered with white ash. Pile the coals on one side of the grill. Set an aluminum foil drip pan in the empty space next to the coals. The pan should be as large as the slab of ribs.

Set the ribs over the drip pan. Cover the grill and let the ribs cook for 40 to 50 minutes, turning them once, until the bone extension equals a minimum of ¼ inch or the internal temperature reaches 180°F—whichever comes first. Brush the ribs with ¼ cup of the glaze. Cover and cook for 10 to 15 minutes longer. Turn the ribs over and brush with the remaining ¼ cup of glaze. Cover and cook for 10 to 15 minutes longer until the ribs are fork-tender.

Heat the reserved 1½ cups of glaze until hot. Serve alongside the ribs.

Hurry Yup BBQ Ribs

(thanks to Frank Simonetti)

Serves 4

Country-style ribs are from the fatty end of the loin and resemble small pork chops. They taste great grilled, but to make the cooking process easy, first cook them on top of the stove and then finish them off over the hot coals. Besides being a great friend, Frank is a cook's cook. His recipes are good . . . great . . . phenomenal! Trust me.

½   cup packed dark brown sugar
¼   cup Dijon mustard or
    Willingham's Old Phartz Mustard
2   12-ounce cans beer or 3 cups
     apple juice
1 teaspoon hot pepper sauce

3   pounds country-style pork or
     beef ribs
2   cups Hurry Yup BBQ Sauce
     (page 168) or W'ham Sweet 'n
     Sassy Sauce

In a large pot, combine the sugar, mustard, beer, and hot pepper sauce and cook over high heat for about 10 minutes until boiling. Add the ribs, cover, reduce the heat to low, and cook for 40 to 50 minutes until the ribs are tender when pierced with a fork.

Prepare the grill. Ignite the coals and let them burn until covered with white ash.

Heat the barbecue sauce in a small saucepan and cover to keep warm.

Lift the ribs from the pot and brush them with the warm sauce. Grill for 12 to 15 minutes, brushing frequently with sauce and turning several times until cooked through and well browned.

Bring the sauce remaining in the saucepan to a boil over medium-high heat and cook for 3 to 5 minutes. Serve the sauce with the ribs.

Pork Apple Kabobs

(thanks to Birgit Andes)

Serves 4

I've know Birgit since she was a pup. She's a darn good cook! This is a terrific dish in the fall when the apples are crisp and tart but it's still warm enough to fire up the grill and cook outside. I like it with steamed white rice. Use lean pork, such as the meat from the loin.

1 cup apple juice

1 tablespoon soy sauce

¼ teaspoon ground ginger

¼ teaspoon ground cloves

¼ teaspoon freshly ground black pepper

1½ to 2 pounds boneless pork, trimmed and cut into 1½-inch cubes

2 to 3 tart apples, cored and cut into wedges

In a large bowl, combine the apple juice, soy sauce, ginger, cloves, and pepper. Add the pork and marinate for at least 4 hours or up to 12 hours.

Prepare the grill. Ignite the coals and let them burn until covered with white ash.

Thread the pork on skewers, alternating with apple wedges. Do not crowd the skewers. Grill for 3 minutes and then rotate each skewer a quarter turn. Grill for 12 to 15 minutes longer, turning the skewers a quarter turn every 3 to 4 minutes, until the pork is cooked through. Remove the meat and apples from the skewers and serve.

Five-gallon containers make great storage, travel, and dispensing containers for water, sauces, seasonings, paper or plastic plates or anything round. Also, if you cut a hole in the side large enough for a hand, you can reach right in and take out napkins.

Grilled Veal Kabobs

(pure Willingham)

Serves 4

These kabobs are meat only. The secret to their excellence is that they are basted almost constantly during cooking so that they absorb lots of good flavor and then they are breaded and cooked for only a few minutes more. The breading holds in all their juicy goodness.

Basting Sauce

¾   cup hot water

½   cup warmed red wine vinegar

2   to 3 tablespoons warmed vegetable oil

2   chicken bouillon cubes

Breading Mixture

½   cup fine cracker crumbs

½   cup fine cornflakes crumbs

1   teaspoon salt

1   teaspoon paprika

¾   teaspoon poultry seasoning or ground thyme, or 3 tablespoons Mild Seasoning Mix (page 171) or W'ham Mild Seasoning

Dash of freshly ground black pepper

2   pounds boneless veal, trimmed and cut into 1½-inch cubes

Egg Glaze

1   large egg, lightly beaten

2   tablespoons milk

In a large bowl, combine the water, vinegar, oil, and bouillon cubes and stir until the bouillon cubes dissolve.

In a long, shallow dish or on a serving platter, combine the cracker crumbs, cornflakes crumbs, salt, paprika, seasoning, and pepper. Carefully stir to combine.

Prepare the grill. Ignite the coals and let them burn until covered with white ash.

Thread the veal cubes onto skewers, taking care not to crowd the meat. Using a brush, slather the meat with the basting sauce. Grill for 3 minutes and then rotate each skewer a quarter turn. Grill for 8 to 10 minutes longer, turning the skewers a quarter turn every 3 to 4 minutes and basting frequently, until the veal is almost cooked to the degree you prefer.

Whisk together the egg and milk.

Remove the skewers from the grill and brush the meat with the egg glaze. Roll each skewer in the breading mixture until well coated. Return the skewers to the grill, placing them on the edge of the grill away from the most intense heat. Cook for 4 to 5 minutes longer until the breading is golden and firm. Remove the meat from the skewers and serve.

He could talk a dog off a meat wagon.

—Steve Uliss

Grilled Poor Man's Cordon Bleu

(pure Willingham)

Serves 6

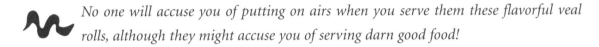 *No one will accuse you of putting on airs when you serve them these flavorful veal rolls, although they might accuse you of serving darn good food!*

½ cup shredded sharp American cheese

¼ cup drained pickle relish

¼ cup chopped pimiento-stuffed green olives

6 ¼-inch veal cutlets

2 tablespoons Mild Seasoning Mix (page 171), W'ham Mild Seasoning, or salt and pepper

6 thin slices pressed chicken

3 thin slices boiled ham, halved

4 tablespoons (½ stick) unsalted butter

2 tablespoons dry sherry

In a small bowl, combine the cheese, relish, and olives to make a spread. Cover and let stand for 30 minutes.

Prepare the grill. Ignite the coals and let them burn until covered with white ash.

Lay the cutlets on the countertop or a wooden cutting board. Cover with waxed paper or plastic wrap. Using a meat mallet or the flat side of a small heavy frying pan, gently flatten the cutlets until about doubled in size. Remove the waxed paper and sprinkle the meat with the seasoning mix.

Lay 1 piece of chicken on each cutlet. Top with a piece of ham. Spread the cheese mixture over the ham and then roll the cutlets up into loose cylinders. Secure each one with toothpicks or tie it at both ends with kitchen twine.

In a small saucepan, melt the butter over medium heat. Add the sherry and whisk just until the butter sauce is heated. Brush the veal rolls with the butter sauce.

Grill over medium-hot coals for 10 to 12 minutes on each side or until the meat is browned and the cheese melts. Baste frequently with the butter sauce during grilling.

Note: *If you prefer, cook the rolls in a well-buttered frying pan for about 30 minutes over low heat, turning frequently to prevent sticking. When you remove the rolls from the pan, add the sherry and more butter, if necessary, to make a sauce to spoon over the veal. Whisk well as the sauce heats.*

When building a charcoal fire in a grill, use enough charcoal so that the bed will be a couple of briquettes deep and spread out about two inches wider than the food cooking above it. Let the coals burn until they are covered with white ash—this means they are good and hot. To test the heat intensity, rely on the old method of holding your hand about six inches over the coals: If you can hold it in place for only two to three seconds, the coals are hot; if you can hold it for up to five seconds, the coals are medium hot; if you can hold it for up to seven seconds, the coals are medium; and if you can hold it for up to ten seconds, the coals are cool.

SEARING —hot coals

GRILLING MOST MEAT AND POULTRY —medium-hot coals

GRILLING VEGETABLES AND DELICATE SEAFOOD —medium coals

WARMING HAMBURGER BUNS, ETC. —cool coals

Grilled Chicken
in-a-Pot

(thanks to Thomas Engel)

Serves 4 to 6

You may never have considered putting a metal pot directly on the grilling grid, but it works. Try cooking chicken this way—when all is said and done, the marinade becomes a thick, sweet sauce for the chicken and rice.

½ cup packed light brown sugar

¼ cup white distilled vinegar

¼ cup soy sauce, All-Purpose Marinade (page 181), or W'ham Marinade

Juice of 1 lemon

1 small onion, finely chopped

¼ cup chopped fresh parsley

1 tablespoon minced garlic

¼ teaspoon ground cumin

¼ teaspoon dried oregano

¼ teaspoon cayenne pepper (optional)

1 3-to 4-pound chicken, cut into pieces

¼ cup chicken broth

2 to 3 cups hot steamed rice

In a large glass or ceramic bowl, combine the sugar, vinegar, soy sauce, lemon juice, onion, parsley, garlic, cumin, oregano, and cayenne, if desired, and stir to mix. Add the chicken and turn the pieces several times in the marinade to coat. Cover and refrigerate for at least 12 hours and up to 16 hours, turning the chicken 2 or 3 times.

Prepare the grill. Ignite the coals and let them burn until covered with white ash.

Transfer the chicken and marinade to a heavy pot with a lid. (Make sure the pot does not have plastic handles or knobs.) Set the pot directly on the grilling grid over the hot coals and cook, stirring the chicken several times, for 20 minutes. Put the cover on the pot and the lid on the grill, open the vents partially, and continue to grill for about 40 minutes until the chicken is almost falling off the bones. Add a few tablespoons of broth if the liquid is evaporating. Add more coals to keep the fire hot, as necessary. Uncover both the grill and the pot and cook for 5 to 8 minutes longer until the sauce is sticky and thick. Serve over rice.

Note: *You may cook the chicken on the stove over medium-high heat, covered, for about 45 minutes. Uncover and cook for 10 to 12 minutes longer until the sauce is sticky and thick.*

Hot Sauce–Marinated Chicken

(thanks to Mike Maness)

Serves 4 to 6

Mike has cooked with me all over the U.S.A. He's a fine artist and has designed our cooking team T-shirts and aprons as well as the menus for my former restaurants. He has an enormous appetite for any food on the BBQ circuit, and has been my friend through thick and thin—which ain't always easy! This dish takes a while, because the cooked chicken should chill before its final heating in the microwave. But this makes it a good make-ahead dish. You can begin with frozen chicken and thaw it in the microwave, already sprinkled with the seasoning mix.

2   pounds boneless, skinless chicken breasts

2   tablespoons Mild Seasoning Mix (page 171) or W'ham Mild Seasoning

Salt to taste

Freshly ground black pepper to taste

1   cup Hot Bar-B-Q Sauce (page 157) or W'ham Cajun Sauce or W'ham Hot Sauce

1   cup shredded Monterey Jack cheese

continued

Sprinkle the chicken breasts with the seasoning mix and salt and pepper. Lay them in a shallow glass or ceramic bowl and cover them with sauce. Turn to coat them evenly. Cover and refrigerate for 2 hours.

Prepare the grill. Ignite the coals and let them burn until covered with white ash.

Lift the chicken breasts from the marinade and grill for about 6 minutes. Turn them, slather them with the marinating sauce, and grill for 5 to 6 minutes longer until they are cooked.

Let the chicken breasts cool, put them in a shallow dish, cover, and refrigerate for at least 2 hours or up to 8 hours, until chilled.

Let the chicken breasts return to room temperature. Lay them in a microwave-safe dish. Sprinkle them with the cheese and microwave on high (100 percent) power for 3 minutes until the cheese melts and the chicken breasts are warm. Serve immediately.

Note: *For a terrific appetizer, cut the chilled, cooked chicken breasts into bite-sized pieces before sprinkling with cheese and microwaving. Spear them with toothpicks and serve.*

Dancing Chicken

(thanks to John Prentice)

Serves 3 to 4

Bet you never heard of this one! The chicken is cooked with the beer can actually inside the bird's cavity. Of course, it's important first to empty the can of half of its beer (I can think of a good way to accomplish that!) because otherwise the can might explode during cooking. The result is chicken that is tender, juicy, and delicious tasting—like you've never tasted before.

1	3-pound chicken	½	teaspoon garlic salt
3	tablespoons Mild Seasoning Mix (page 171) or W'ham Mild Seasoning	1	12-ounce can beer

Prepare the grill. Ignite the coals and let them burn until covered with white ash.

Wash the chicken inside and out and, while it's still damp, rub it with the seasoning mix inside and out. Sprinkle the garlic salt lightly over the chicken.

Fold the neck skin down and fasten it to the breast with a toothpick. Drink (or pour out) about a third of the beer. Insert the partially full can of beer, open (pop-top) end facing out, into the cavity of the chicken.

Grill the chicken, breast side up, over medium-hot coals, positioning the chicken so that it is not directly over the coals. Cover the grill and open the vents partially. Grill for 1½ to 2 hours until the skin cracks and the legs and wings are easy to pull from the body. Using tongs or a thick oven mitt, remove the beer can before serving the chicken.

Note: *You can roast the chicken in a 350°F oven for 2 to 2½ hours instead of grilling it.*

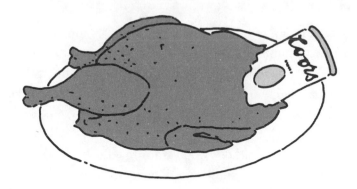

Marinated Chicken Breasts

(thanks to Carolyn Wells)

Serves 6

I have been attending and competing in the American Royal barbecue contest since 1984 and I can tell you without question that without this lady, the American Royal would be sorely lacking. She and her husband, Gary, are truly a major ingredient in the life of barbecue. You can never go wrong with this simple recipe for marinated chicken breasts. Everyone loves their immediately recognizable and predictably satisfying flavor.

¾ cup white wine vinegar	2 tablespoons chili powder
2 tablespoons water	1 teaspoon freshly ground black pepper
2 tablespoons freshly squeezed lemon juice	½ teaspoon salt
1 tablespoon vegetable oil	6 chicken breast halves, bone in

In a small glass bowl or jar, combine the vinegar, water, lemon juice, oil, chili powder, pepper, and salt. Stir or shake to combine.

Wash the chicken breasts and pat them dry with paper towels. Put the breasts in a heavy-duty, self-sealing plastic bag and pour in the marinade. Seal the bag and shake gently to coat the chicken with marinade. Put the bag in a bowl and refrigerate for 2 hours. Turn the chicken occasionally during marinating.

Soak about 1 cup of apple or hickory wood chips in a bucket of water for about 1 hour.

Prepare the grill. Ignite the coals and let them burn until covered with white ash.

Push the hot coals to the side of the grill and position a drip pan in the center of the grill, surrounded by coals. Sprinkle the wood chips over the coals.

Drain the chicken and reserve the marinade. Put the chicken breasts, skin side up, over the drip pan, cover the grill, open the vents, and grill for 35 to 45 minutes, or until the juices run clear when the thickest part of the largest breast is pierced with a fork. Brush the breasts with the marinade several times during the first 15 to 20 minutes of grilling.

Self-sealing plastic bags are great for marinating chicken breasts. This makes it easy to massage the meat in the marinade, to "slush it around" without getting your hands messy. Even better, you can put several different pieces of meat in a number of bags and pack them in the cooler to carry to the backyard grill, a picnic site, or a barbecue contest. Or just to store in the refrigerator.

Grilled Italian Herb Chicken Breasts

(thanks to Wyn Bellerjeau)

Serves 4

Wyn is one of the finer judges on the barbecue circuit. He's given greatly to the sport! And his recipe for chicken is another straightforward and delicious way to marinate chicken breasts. This time, the chicken is boneless and skinless, so it grills in a jiffy.

4 boneless, skinless chicken breasts

½ cup bottled Italian salad dressing or ¼ cup bottled Italian salad dressing and ¼ cup dry white wine

1 tablespoon Italian seasoning

1 tablespoon lemon-pepper seasoning

1 teaspoon powdered butter sprinkles

½ teaspoon garlic powder

continued

Place the chicken breasts in a shallow glass or ceramic dish. Add the ½ cup salad dressing. Turn the breasts to coat. Sprinkle each breast with Italian seasoning, lemon-pepper seasoning, butter sprinkles, and garlic powder. Use your fingertips to rub the seasoning into the meat. Cover and refrigerate for 2 to 3 hours.

Prepare the grill. Ignite the coals and let them burn until covered with white ash.

Grill the chicken breasts for about 6 minutes on each side, brushing with the marinade several times. Serve immediately.

If you are looking for a helping hand, look no farther
than the end of your own sleeve.
—my neighbor, Jerry Ruden

BBQ Swordfish

(thanks to Steve Uliss)

Serves 2

I don't hold it against Steve that he's from Boston, and although he's still having difficulty learning the language of Southern Barbecue, he knows swordfish! Swordfish is one of the best fish to grill—and with a good dry rub seasoning the succulent meat, it's dynamite.

2 tablespoons Mild Seasoning Mix (page 171) or W'ham Mild Seasoning	4 tablespoons (½ stick) melted butter
2 6- to 7-ounce center-cut swordfish steaks	Lemon wedges, for garnish

Sprinkle the seasoning over the swordfish and, using your fingertips, rub it gently into the flesh. Let the fish sit at room temperature for 20 minutes.

Prepare the grill. Ignite the coals and let them burn until covered with white ash. Oil the grilling grid.

Grill the steaks for about 6 minutes on each side until almost flaking and opaque. Brush with melted butter just before removing from the grill and serve immediately, with lemon wedges for garnish.

Herbed Shrimp with Basil

(thanks to Dr. Dick Reynolds)

Serves 4

What can I say but "thanks, Doc!" for creating a dish fit for predinner, a main course, or a late-night snack? Nothing beats grilled shrimp and this is a surefire way to please everyone who appreciates them. I suggest jumbo shrimp so they won't slip through the grilling grid, but if you have a fine-mesh grilling basket or grilling grid, use slightly smaller shrimp if you prefer.

2	pounds jumbo shrimp in the shell	1	tablespoon chopped parsley
¾	cup olive oil	1	teaspoon salt
2	tablespoons freshly squeezed lemon juice	½	teaspoon oregano
2	cups chopped fresh basil	½	teaspoon freshly ground black pepper
2	garlic cloves, crushed		

Peel and devein the shrimp and lay them in a single layer in a shallow glass or ceramic dish.

In a food processor fitted with the metal blade, blend the olive oil with the lemon juice, basil, garlic, parsley, salt, oregano, and pepper until smooth. Pour the marinade over the shrimp. Cover and refrigerate for 2 hours. Stir the shrimp 4 or 5 times during marinating.

Prepare the grill. Ignite the coals and let them burn until covered with white ash. Lightly oil the grilling grid.

Lay the shrimp on the oiled grilling grid over medium-hot coals and grill for 3 to 5 minutes on each side until slightly charred and cooked through. Do not overcook. Serve immediately.

Grilled Shrimp with BBQ Sauce

(thanks to Les Kincaid)

Serves 4

Les and I have never met face-to-face, but I often talk with him on his radio show aired from Las Vegas. You may have heard him on the air, bragging about his culinary masterpieces. This recipe is a case in point. Shrimp grill in a flash, so have the salt and lemon juice ready for seasoning them hot off the grill—and the folks ready to devour these beauties.

1½ pounds large shrimp in the shell
2 cups Sweet Bar-B-Q Sauce (page 158) or W'ham Sweet 'n Sassy Sauce

⅓ cup vegetable oil
½ teaspoon salt
⅓ cup freshly squeezed lemon juice

Peel and devein the shrimp.

Put the shrimp into a glass or ceramic bowl and add the sauce and oil. Cover and refrigerate for 1 hour.

Prepare the grill. Ignite the coals and let them burn until covered with white ash. Lightly oil the grilling grid.

Lift the shrimp from the marinade and shake most of it off. Thread the shrimp on metal skewers and grill them for 2 to 3 minutes to a side, basting frequently with the marinade.

Remove the shrimp from the skewers and pile them on a serving platter. Sprinkle them with salt and lemon juice and serve immediately.

South City Shrimp

(thanks to Steve Prentiss)

Serves 4

Steve is like a son to me—and typically he does his own thing. These shrimp are something he does great! The bacon gives the shrimp a deliciously smoky flavor and adds moisture and certain irresistibility!

1½ pounds jumbo shrimp in the shell	2 tablespoons fajita seasoning
1 cup water	¾ pound thin-sliced bacon
¼ cup Rose's lime juice	8 tablespoons (1 stick) butter
1 cup chopped pickled jalapeño peppers, drained	1 fresh jalapeño pepper, seeded and chopped
2 tablespoons Mild Seasoning Mix (page 171) or W'ham Mild Seasoning	

Peel and devein the shrimp.

In a large glass or ceramic bowl, combine the water, lime juice, pickled jalapeños, seasoning mix, and fajita seasoning. Add the shrimp and toss to coat. Cover and refrigerate for 1 to 2 hours.

Put about 30 wooden toothpicks in a small bowl and cover them with water. Let them soak until ready to use.

Prepare the grill. Ignite the coals and let them burn until covered with white ash. Oil the grilling grid.

Lift the shrimp from the marinade one at a time and wrap each one in a slice of bacon. Secure the bacon with a soaked toothpick. Lay all the wrapped shrimp on a baking sheet.

Meanwhile, put the butter and jalapeño pepper in a small saucepan and heat over medium heat until the butter is melted. Cover to keep warm.

Lay the shrimp on the oiled grilling grid over medium-hot coals and grill for 3 to 5 minutes on each side until the bacon is browned and crispy. Brush often with the jalapeño butter. Do not overcook. Serve immediately.

7

Down-Home Chicken, Fish, and Seafood

Tennessee Mountain Fried Chicken · Chicken and Vegetable Noodle Casserole · Lemon Chicken · Southern Fried Fish · Tennessee Fried Fish · W'ham Baked Shrimp · Catfish with Mustard Sauce · Trout Blue · W'ham Bam Blackened Fish

Even the most ardent 'cuer and enthusiastic backyard griller turn to the kitchen every now and then to prepare dishes that can't be cooked in a barbecue cooker or over a hot grill. Some of the best food to come out of the South originated in home kitchens or over camp-fires. I call this down-home cooking, meaning the dishes here are just plain good, simple, straightforward Southern home cooking.

Fried chicken is about as Southern as it gets, and I could not put together a cookbook of Southern recipes without including my favorite recipe. Fried fish is a Southern tradition too, which began in the days when fish were pulled from farm ponds and mountain streams and then cooked right then and there over a blazing campfire or carried home and immediately fried up in a big black cast-iron skillet. I usually deep-fry fish now—try the Tennessee Fried Fish, Southern Fried Fish, or Catfish with Mustard Sauce. Admittedly, these can't replace barbecue in my affec-tions, but I sure do like them once in a while.

Tennessee Mountain Fried Chicken

(pure Willingham)

Serves 6 to 8

What's a cookbook from the South without a recipe for fried chicken? As long as the oil is good and hot, frying is easy—and the chicken is oh-so-delicious. This breading is great for dusting onion rings too.

3 cups all-purpose flour	2 3-pound frying chickens, cut up
3 tablespoons Mild Seasoning Mix (page 171) or W'ham Mild Seasoning	Vegetable oil, for frying
	About ⅔ cup bacon drippings

In a large shallow bowl or pan, mix the flour and seasoning mix. Lay a few pieces of chicken in the mixture and turn to coat on all sides. Set them on a waxed paper–lined baking sheet while coating the remaining pieces of chicken.

Pour the vegetable oil and bacon drippings into a deep, heavy frying pan to a depth of 3 to 3½ inches or into a deep-fat fryer and heat it to 350°F.

Fry the chicken, a few pieces at a time, for about 15 minutes, turning several times, until crispy and browned. Remove them and drain on paper towels. Cover them loosely with foil to keep warm. Continue frying until all the chicken is cooked, letting the oil return to 350°F between each batch. Serve as soon as all the chicken is cooked.

Don't confuse me with the facts. My mind is made up already!

Chicken and Vegetable Noodle Casserole

(thanks to Darlene Ryan)

Serves 6 to 8

Darlene, pronounced "Darlin'," don't cut her husband Rex's grass—and he's afraid to ask her in case she stops cookin'! Have some leftover chicken? Use it to make this easy-as-one-two-three casserole. Or start with a two-and-a-half-pound split fryer, baked, grilled, or poached, and use the cooked meat to make the dish. Either way, it's great!

8	tablespoons (1 stick) butter or margarine	2	cups drained canned tomatoes
2	small onions, chopped	2	cups cubed cooked chicken
2	green bell peppers, seeded and chopped	2	cups cubed American cheese, such as Velveeta
1	tablespoon Mild Seasoning Mix (page 171) or W'ham Mild Seasoning	2	6-ounce cans mushrooms, drained
		½	cup fresh, defrosted frozen, or canned peas
2½	cups chicken broth	12	ounces dried vermicelli, cooked and drained

In a large skillet, melt the butter over medium-high heat. Add the onions and cook for 2 to 3 minutes, stirring, until softened. Add the peppers and cook, stirring, for 4 to 5 minutes longer until softened. Add the seasoning mix and stir well.

In a flameproof casserole, combine the broth, tomatoes, chicken, and cheese. Cook over medium heat, stirring, until the cheese melts. Add the mushrooms and peas and cook for 2 to 3 minutes longer to heat through. Add the vegetables from the skillet and stir to mix. Cook over medium-high heat for about 5 minutes until the flavors blend and the casserole is hot.

Add the pasta, stir well, and cook for 3 to 4 minutes longer until the mixture is bubbling hot. Serve immediately.

Lemon Chicken

(thanks to Darlene Ryan)

Serves 4

 Boneless, skinless chicken breasts cook in minutes.

3	tablespoons all-purpose flour	1	tablespoon butter or margarine
¾	teaspoon Mild Seasoning Mix (page 171) or W'ham Seasoning Mix	1	onion, chopped
		1	cup chicken broth
4	boneless, skinless chicken breast halves	3	tablespoons freshly squeezed lemon juice
2	tablespoons olive oil	½	teaspoon dried thyme
		1	tablespoon fresh parsley

Put the flour and seasoning mix in a paper or plastic bag. Put the chicken in the bag and shake to coat.

In a large skillet, heat the oil over medium-high heat. Add the chicken (reserve the flour mixture in the bag) and cook, turning, for 2 to 3 minutes to brown on both sides. Transfer the chicken to a plate and set aside.

Add the butter to the skillet and heat until melted. Add the onion and cook, stirring, for 4 to 5 minutes until softened. Add the reserved flour and stir until smooth. Add the broth, lemon juice, and thyme, raise the heat, and bring to a boil.

Return the chicken to the pan. Reduce the heat to medium, cover, and cook for 8 to 10 minutes until the chicken is cooked through and tender. Spoon the sauce over the chicken, sprinkle it with parsley, and serve immediately.

Southern Fried Fish

(thanks to Joe Ketcham)

Serves 6 to 8

Hum or whistle "Shake, Rattle, and Roll!" or "Sweet Georgia Brown" when you're shaking the fish fillets in the paper bag filled with breading. It helps! Serve this with Brownwood-Style Coleslaw (page 137), wedges of lemon, wedges of sweet onions, ketchup, Hush Dem Puppies (page 37), French fries, or chunks of Cheddar cheese.

8   6- to 8-ounce freshwater fish fillets, such as bass, catfish, crappie, walleye, or bream

2   8- to 10-ounce bottles mild hot pepper sauce, such as Louisiana Southern Spice Hot Sauce

½   cup dried Italian-style bread crumbs

2   cups yellow cornmeal

1   tablespoon freshly ground black pepper

1½   tablespoons Mild Seasoning Mix (page 171), W'ham Mild Seasoning, or Tony Chachère's creole seasoning

½   teaspoon seasoned salt, such as Lawry's Seasoned Salt

Pinch of cayenne pepper

Peanut oil, for frying

Lay the fish fillets in a shallow glass or ceramic dish and add the pepper sauce. Cover and refrigerate for 2 to 3 hours.

Put the bread crumbs in a blender and process until finely ground. Transfer the bread crumbs to a paper bag. Add the cornmeal, black pepper, seasoning mix, seasoned salt, and cayenne. Fold the bag closed and shake to blend. Taste and adjust the seasonings as desired.

Lift the fish from the marinade and shake gently to remove excess. Put 2 to 3 fillets in the bag, fold closed, and shake to coat. Remove and lay the breaded fish on a wax paper–lined baking sheet. Continue until all the fillets are breaded.

Pour the peanut oil into a deep heavy frying pan to a depth of 3 to 3½ inches or into a deep-fat fryer and heat to 400°F.

Using tongs, gently lay 2 to 3 fillets in the oil and fry for 2 to 3 minutes, turning the fillets twice once they rise to the surface of the oil. The fish is done after the second turn, or when the flesh is opaque and flakes. Remove and drain on paper towels. Cover loosely with foil to keep warm. Continue frying until all the fish is cooked, letting the oil return to 400°F between each batch. Serve immediately.

Put vegetable oil used for cooking in a squeezable mustard or ketchup dispenser. This is handy for adding a little oil as you fry, easier to use than bulky bottles, and a heck of a lot safer.

Tennessee Fried Fish

(pure Willingham)

Serves 4

Frying fish is a Southern tradition—no one does it better than folks from these parts. You can keep the fish in a warm oven while frying it all up, although there's a good chance it will get snatched as soon as it's cool enough to grab!

1	large egg	3	cups yellow cornmeal
9	tablespoons Mild Seasoning Mix (page 171) or W'ham Mild Seasoning		Vegetable oil, for frying
4	cups milk		
2	pounds freshwater fish fillets, such as bass, catfish, crappie, sunfish, or bream		

Whisk the egg, 1 tablespoon seasoning, and milk together in a shallow bowl. Soak the fillets in the mixture for about 20 minutes.

Preheat the oven to 200°F.

Combine the remaining seasoning mix and cornmeal in a paper or plastic bag. Lift the fillets from the milk and put them, a fillet at a time, in the bag, shaking to coat on both sides. As each fillet is coated, lay it on a waxed paper–lined baking sheet.

Pour oil into a deep-fat fryer or into a large heavy frying pan to a depth of 2 inches. Heat over high heat until the oil reaches 375°F. Using tongs, put 2 or 3 fillets in the oil and fry for 2 to 3 minutes, turning once or twice, until crispy brown. Do not crowd the pan. Remove the fillets from the oil and drain on paper towels. If frying in batches, let the oil return to 375°F between each one.

Put the fillets in the warm oven while frying the rest or serve immediately.

W'ham Baked
Shrimp

(thanks to Marge Willingham)

Serves 6

Line the picnic or kitchen table with newspaper and then bake up some shrimp. Everyone peels his or her own—and everyone has a great time and great eats. The Cajun seasoning will make spicier shrimp. Down South, where we've elevated casual eating and good times to an art form, spreading newspaper on the table makes perfect sense—no clean up! My wife, Marge ("Marge in Charge"), insists on the newspaper!

pounds unshelled large shrimp	10 to 12 slices French bread
1½ cups (3 sticks) butter or margarine	
2 to 4 tablespoons Mild Seasoning Mix (page 171) or W'ham Mild Seasoning, or Cajun Seasoning Mix (page 172), or W'ham Cajun Hot Seasoning, or more to taste	

Preheat the oven to 350°F.

Spread the shrimp in a single layer on a rimmed baking sheet or other shallow baking pan. Dot with butter and sprinkle generously with seasoning.

Bake for 10 to 12 minutes until the shrimp turn pink.

Serve right from the pan, shelling the shrimp as you go and dipping the bread and shrimp in the pan juices.

Catfish with Mustard Sauce

(thanks to Dr. Dick Reynolds)

Serves 4

 The oniony, creamy mustard sauce tastes great with mild fried catfish.

Mustard Sauce

2 tablespoons (¼ stick) unsalted butter	½ cup chopped parsley
¾ cup finely chopped onion	2 tablespoons Dijon mustard or Willingham's Old Phartz Mustard
½ cup dry white wine	Salt to taste
1 cup heavy cream	Freshly ground black pepper to taste

Catfish

½ cup all-purpose flour	Freshly ground black pepper to taste
½ cup cornmeal	2 pounds catfish fillets
Salt to taste	Vegetable oil, for frying

Preheat the oven to 225°F.

To make the sauce, in a large sauté pan, melt the butter over low heat and sauté the onion for 3 to 4 minutes until softened.

Add the wine and cook over medium heat for about 5 minutes until the liquid evaporates. Add the cream and cook for 3 to 4 minutes until reduced by a quarter.

Remove the pan from the heat and stir in the parsley, mustard, salt, and pepper. Cover to keep warm and set aside.

To prepare the fish, whisk the flour and cornmeal together and season with salt and pepper. Spread in a shallow dish. Lay the fish in the coating mixture, turning to coat well on both sides.

Pour oil into a deep-fat fryer or a large heavy frying pan to a depth of 2 inches. Heat over high heat until the oil reaches 370°F. Using tongs, put 2 or 3 fillets in the oil and fry for 2 to 3 minutes, turning once or twice, until crispy brown. Do not crowd the pan. Remove the fish from the oil and drain on paper towels. If frying in batches, let the oil return to 370°F between each one. Keep the fish warm in the oven until all are fried.

Reheat the sauce if necessary. Serve the fish with the warm sauce.

> *To remove fish or onion odor from your hands, utensils, and dish cloths, dilute a teaspoon of baking powder in a quart of water and rinse whatever in this water. Celery juice and lemon juice help too.*

Trout Blue
(thanks to Tom and Joanie Carlisle)

Serves 2

My old friend Tom Carlisle taught me to recognize good food—and to spot hypocrisy. I once asked him how I could repay his kindness and he said, "By being my friend, John, which ain't easy." He meant I had to accept him as he was: rough and scratchy. Tom taught me to like trout and lamb, and influenced my cooking style considerably. Rest easy, friend. Use the freshest trout you can catch or buy (never use frozen for this preparation) and handle the fresh fish as little and as carefully as you can. You can substitute other freshwater fish too, such as bass, catfish, walleye, and perch.

2	12-ounce trout, with head and skin	8	tablespoons (1 stick) unsalted butter or margarine
1	cup All-Purpose Marinade (page 181) or W'ham Marinade, or soy sauce	1	teaspoon salt
		1	tablespoon toasted sliced almonds
		1	tablespoon vermouth per 1 cup water used for cooking the trout

Rinse the trout inside and out and gently pat dry. Pour the marinade in a glass or ceramic bowl large enough to hold the trout. Put the trout in the bowl, spoon the marinade over them several times, remembering to spoon some into the interior cavity. Transfer the trout to a shallow glass or ceramic dish, cover, and refrigerate for at least 30 minutes and for no longer than 1 hour.

In a small saucepan, melt the butter over medium heat. Stir in the salt and sliced almonds until just mixed and the almonds are coated with butter. Using a slotted spoon, lift the almonds from the sauce and transfer them to a skillet. Set aside the butter sauce.

Cook the almonds over medium-high heat for 5 to 8 minutes until lightly browned and tender but not brittle. Set aside.

Add water to a poaching pan, saucepan, or deep skillet to a depth of 2½ to 3 inches. Measure the water, adding a tablespoon of vermouth for every cup. Bring to a brisk simmer. Add the trout in the "swimming" position and poach over medium-high heat, never letting the poaching liquid boil, until the eyes turn blue.

Lift the fish from the pan, brush them with the butter sauce, and serve them sprinkled with almonds.

W'ham Bam
Blackened Fish

(pure Willingham)

Serves 4

This recipe is so darn simple you may not think it's worth bothering. But if you like blackened anything, try this! The seasoning mix leaves a savory, blackened crust on the fish.

12 tablespoons (1½ sticks) butter or margarine

2 pounds freshwater fish fillets, such as bass, catfish, crappie, sunfish, or bream

Mild Seasoning Mix (page 171) or W'ham Mild Seasoning

In a large skillet, melt 8 tablespoons of the butter over medium heat. Remove the skillet from the heat and lay the fish fillets in the butter, turning to coat. Lay the fillets on a work surface and sprinkle liberally on both sides with seasoning mix. Transfer them to a shallow dish, cover, and refrigerate for 1 hour (no longer).

Melt the remaining 4 tablespoons of butter in a large heavy, well-seasoned skillet over high heat. When bubbling hot, add the fillets and cook for 2 to 3 minutes on a side until blackened. Serve immediately.

If you go boating or fishing on a lake, attach a large cork to your key chain. This way, if your keys are accidently dropped in the water, they will be easy to retrieve.

8

Beans and Chilis

Sweet 'n' Sassy Beans · Red Beans and Rice with Kielbasa ·
Happy Hawg Beans · Tammy's Baked Beans · Beans and Rice
for a Crowd · Y'all Come Down Chili · Country Chili ·
Chili—Hot! Hot! Hot!

Barbecue is mighty fine eaten all by its lonesome, with nothing more to accompany it than a little sauce. But why leave it to fly solo? Most folks like some other food to eat alongside the barbecue—it makes it more of a meal. And beans are one of the most popular side dishes down South. Of course, they also make a good main course—so try these recipes even if you haven't cooked barbecue.

Chili, too, is a great main course dish—everybody loves a good chili with character and you can make it as mild or hot as you like. Chili is a welcome guest at a backyard potluck or church picnic. Bring a big pot, set it on the table with the rest of the food, and watch it disappear.

Sweet 'n' Sassy Beans

(pure Willingham)

Serves 8 to 10

Here's an example of taking a store-bought product—plain-as-dirt canned pork and beans—and fancying it up to make a meal worth eating. My choice of beans is Bush's Best Baked Beans, but you can choose your own favorite. If you decide to bake this hearty casserole in a conventional oven, you can add the liquid smoke for flavor. If using your smoker or cooker, forget the liquid smoke; you've got the real thing and you'll get better, fuller flavor.

¼ pound breakfast sausage or bacon, crumbled

¼ cup diced onion

¼ pound pulled or chopped Bar-B-Q'd Pork Shoulder (page 42) or smoked pork butt

4 16-ounce cans store-bought pork and beans

¼ cup Sweet Bar-B-Q Sauce (page 158) or W'ham Sweet 'n Sassy Sauce

½ cup molasses

1½ tablespoons Mild Seasoning Mix (page 171) or W'ham Mild Seasoning

½ teaspoon liquid smoke (optional)

Start the cooker (pages 11–13), allowing it to reach a temperature of 250°F, or preheat the oven to 350°F.

In a large skillet, cook the sausage and onion over medium-high heat for 5 to 6 minutes until the sausage is browned and the onion softened. Add the pork and cook for 2 to 3 minutes longer until the meat is just heated through. Set aside.

In a large bowl, combine the pork and beans, sauce, molasses, seasoning mix, and liquid smoke, if using. Stir well and transfer to a deep casserole. The casserole should be large enough hold the mixture so that it is no deeper than 4 inches and no shallower than 2 inches. Add the sausage-pork mixture and stir well.

Cook in the cooker, uncovered, for 3½ hours, or in the oven, covered, for 2½ hours until hot and bubbling and the flavors are well blended.

Red Beans and Rice with Kielbasa

(thanks to Sandra L. Shultz)

Serves 4 as a main dish;
8 to 10 as a side dish

As a working mother, Sandra relies on this quickie dish when time and tempers get short. It's an old reliable. The spicy kielbasa sausage is made hotter with the seasoning mix—great! Use another kind of sausage if you prefer.

2   16-ounce cans red kidney beans
1   pound kielbasa sausage, cut into
    bite-sized pieces
1½ teaspoons Cajun Seasoning Mix
    (page 172) or W'ham Cajun Hot
    Seasoning

1   teaspoon Hot Seasoning Mix
    (page 173) or W'ham Hot Stuff
    Seasoning
2   cups hot cooked rice

In a large skillet, heat the beans and their juice over medium heat. When they are heated through, add the sausage and seasoning mixes. Stir and cook, uncovered, for 15 to 20 minutes until the beans and sausage are tender and bubbling hot. Serve over the cooked rice.

Three large celery stalks added to about two cups of beans (navy, red, pinto, etc.) will make them easier to digest. So will a bit of baking soda added to the cooking liquid.

Hot chile peppers can inflict bodily harm—rashes and red, stinging eyes—if you don't take precautions. For this reason, it's advisable to wear rubber or latex gloves when cutting up jalapeños, habaneros, or any hot chile pepper. Even after the chile peppers are chopped and you remove the gloves, wash your hands in warm soapy water to wash away any residue.

Begin by rinsing the chile peppers in cold water. Split them and remove the seeds. The dangerous "heat" is in the seeds. Chop hot chile peppers separately from mild bell peppers. If even a few seeds from a hot chile pepper get mixed in with those of a milder pepper, you can have a lot of "fire" on your hands, or in your mouth or, worse in your eyes.

Happy Hawg Beans

(thanks to Dr. James M. Stalker)

Serves 12 to 14

Besides being a fine surgeon, Doc Stalker is a true-blue barbecue aficionado who builds his own cookers, makes his own sauce and ribs. His beans are great too. If you're feeding a big crowd, double or triple this recipe—it works great. Add mild canned chile pepper or canned mushrooms for variety, if you like them.

2	pounds dried pinto beans	1	teaspoon ground cumin
1	tablespoon beef bouillon granules	2	tablespoons sugar
1	small onion, chopped	1	tablespoon castor oil (optional)
2	green bell peppers, seeded and chopped	2	to 3 teaspoons salt
2	garlic cloves, minced	¼	pound pulled or chopped Bar-B-Q'd Pork Shoulder (page 42), smoked pork butt, or crumbled country sausage
1	fresh jalapeño or habanero chile, seeded and chopped		

Put the beans in a large pot and add enough water to cover by a depth of 2 to 3 inches. Let the beans soak for at least 6 hours and up to 8 hours, changing the water 2 to 3 times during soaking. Drain, rinse the beans, and return them to the pot.

Cover the beans with water to a depth of 2 inches and bring them to a boil, partially covered, over high heat. Reduce the heat to a low simmer, skim the foam from the surface of the beans, and add the bouillon granules, onion, green peppers, garlic, jalapeño, cumin, sugar, and castor oil, if desired. Cook for about 2 hours until the beans and vegetables are tender. Taste and season with salt.

Add the pork and cook for 10 to 15 minutes until it is heated through. Adjust the seasoning and serve immediately.

Note: *Castor oil supposedly alleviates gas and indigestion often caused by beans.*

Instant potato flakes make a good thickener for stews, beans, and other one-pot dishes.

Tammy's Baked Beans

(thanks to Les Kincaid)

Serves 4

This is one of my favorite side dishes to serve with grilled or slow-cooked foods. It's a good choice to tote along for a potluck too.

4	strips of bacon	¾	cup ketchup
2	red onions, finely chopped	1	tablespoon chili powder
1	garlic clove, minced	1	teaspoon dry mustard
1	16-ounce can baked beans	½	teaspoon freshly ground white
1	cup packed dark brown sugar		pepper

Preheat the oven to 325°F.

In a skillet, cook the bacon over medium-high heat for 3 to 4 minutes until crisp. Drain on a paper towel and when it is cool, break it into small pieces. Pour off all but 1 tablespoon of the drippings.

Add the onions and cook for 2 to 3 minutes until softened. Add the garlic and cook for about 2 minutes longer. Transfer to a bowl and add the beans, brown sugar, ketchup, chili powder, mustard, pepper, and bacon. Mix well.

Pour the mixture into a 2-quart baking dish and bake for 2½ hours until hot, browned, and bubbling. Serve immediately.

> Show me your friends and I will show you what you are.

Beans and Rice for a Crowd

(thanks to Buddy Lyons)

Serves 18 to 20

When the gang's all there, try this as a side dish or main course. Either way it's terrific! The addition of the potatoes makes it especially hearty when spooned over rice.

3   pounds chorizo, kielbasa, or other spicy sausage, crumbled

1   pound baked ham, thinly sliced and julienned

4   green bell peppers, seeded and chopped

2   large onions, chopped

2   garlic cloves, minced

2   quarts (8 cups) water

2   28-ounce cans tomatoes, with their juice

5   large fresh tomatoes, chopped

8   bay leaves

2   tablespoons Cajun Seasoning Mix (page 172) or W'ham Cajun Hot Seasoning

1½ pounds baking potatoes, baked, cooled, peeled, and cubed

9 to 10 cups hot cooked rice

In a large skillet, brown the sausage and ham over medium-high heat. Transfer them to a bowl and set aside. Drain all but 1 tablespoon of the fat from the skillet. Add the peppers and onions and cook for about 5 minutes until softened. Add the garlic and cook for about 2 minutes longer. Transfer them to the bowl of meat and stir to mix.

In a large stockpot, combine the water, tomatoes and juice, chopped tomatoes, bay leaves, and seasoning mix. Bring to a simmer over high heat, reduce the heat to medium, and simmer, stirring occasionally, for about 1 hour.

About 20 minutes before the end of cooking, add the potatoes. Stir gently. Before serving, discard the bay leaves. Serve over the hot rice.

Y'all Come Down Chili

(pure Willingham)

Serves 8 to 12

Make up a big pot of this great-tasting chili whenever a crowd is expected. If it's not all scarfed up (fat chance!), freeze the leftovers in small portions for your personal pleasure later on.

3	pounds ground beef	2	10-ounce cans tomatoes or diced
3	large onions, chopped		tomatoes with chiles (Rotel),
8	tablespoons (1 stick) margarine		drained and diced
¼	cup cider vinegar	12	garlic cloves, finely diced
4	tablespoons Mild Seasoning Mix	¼	cup dill pickle juice
	(page 171) or W'ham Mild	4	tablespoons chili powder
	Seasoning		2 to 3 teaspoons Hot Seasoning Mix
3	tablespoons store-bought chili mix		(page 173) or W'ham Hot Stuff
3	16-ounce cans store-bought baked		Seasoning (optional)
	beans		

In a Dutch oven or large pot, brown the ground beef and onions and cook, stirring, for about 15 minutes until the beef is browned. Drain off the fat.

Add the margarine, vinegar, mild seasoning mix, chili mix, beans, and tomatoes and mix well. Add the garlic, pickle juice, and chili powder. Add the hot seasoning mix to taste, if desired.

Bring to a simmer over high heat, reduce the heat to medium-low, and cook gently for 1 hour. Remove from the heat and let the chili sit for 30 minutes before serving. Serve immediately or cool, covered, overnight in the refrigerator and reheat the next day.

Note: *I like to remove about a third of the bean mixture and mash it with a fork, potato masher, or in a blender. I return this to the chili for improved body and texture. It also gives it a wonderful "second-day" full-bodied flavor.*

Country Chili

(thanks to John P. Young)

Serves 8 to 10

The pork sausage gives this chili bold flavor and texture, and the black beans add an unexpected dimension. It's not as "hot" as some of the other chilis in this chapter, but its seasoning is far from timid.

2   pounds lean ground beef
1   pound spicy country pork
    sausage, crumbled
1   medium-sized onion, chopped
1   garlic clove, chopped
1   tablespoon store-bought chili mix
1   10-ounce can tomato sauce
1   10-ounce can tomatoes, chopped
3   tablespoons Mild Seasoning Mix
    (page 171) or W'ham Mild
    Seasoning

1   cup canned red kidney beans, with
    their juice
1   cup canned black beans, with their
    juice
Chopped onion, for garnish
Shredded Monterey Jack cheese, for
    garnish

In a large skillet, cook the ground beef and sausage meat for about 10 minutes over medium-high heat until browned. Break up the meat with a fork or wooden spoon as it cooks. Lift the meat from the pan with a slotted spoon and transfer it to large pot. Drain off all but 1 tablespoon of fat from the skillet.

Add the onion to the skillet and cook, stirring, for 5 to 8 minutes until softened. Add the garlic and cook, stirring, for 2 to 3 minutes longer. Transfer the onion and garlic to the pot with the meat and mix well.

Add the chili mix, tomato sauce, tomatoes, and seasoning mix and stir to combine. Bring to a boil. Immediately reduce the heat to medium-low and simmer, partially covered, for 2½ to 3 hours until the meat is tender and the flavors well blended.

About 30 minutes before the chili is cooked, add the beans. Adjust the seasonings. Serve in shallow bowls, sprinkled with chopped onion and shredded cheese.

Chili—Hot! Hot! Hot!

(thanks to Lex Lyon)

Serves 6

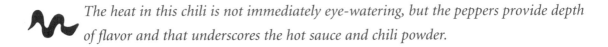 *The heat in this chili is not immediately eye-watering, but the peppers provide depth of flavor and that underscores the hot sauce and chili powder.*

2	pounds ground (beef) chuck	3½	tablespoons chili powder
1	teaspoon salt	3	tablespoons Worcestershire sauce
1	teaspoon freshly ground black pepper	2	large banana peppers, seeded and chopped
1	garlic clove, chopped	2	dashes of hot pepper sauce
1	teaspoon garlic powder	2¼	cups water
1	large red onion, chopped	1	12-ounce can tomato paste
2	celery stalks, including the leaves, chopped	1	15-ounce can tomato sauce
1	red bell pepper, seeded and chopped	2	15-ounce cans red kidney beans, with their juice

In a large skillet, cook the ground beef for about 10 minutes over medium-high heat until browned. Break up the meat with a fork or wooden spoon as it cooks. Season with salt and pepper. Add the garlic and garlic powder, stir to mix, and cook for 2 to 3 minutes longer. Lift the meat from the pan with a slotted spoon and transfer it to a large pot.

Put the onion, celery, and red pepper in a bowl. Sprinkle them with the chili powder and Worcestershire sauce and mix well Add the vegetables to the meat, mix well, and cook over medium-high heat for 30 to 40 minutes until the vegetables begin to soften.

Put the banana pepper, hot pepper sauce, and ¼ cup of the water into a blender. Purée until smooth. Add to the chili and stir well. Add the tomato paste, tomato sauce, beans with their juice, and the remaining 2 cups water. Simmer the chili, partially covered, for about 3 hours longer until the flavors are blended.

9

Fixin's: Vegetable
Side Dishes

W'hammed Corn · Creamed Fennel and Corn · Grilled Herb-
Marinated Vegetables · Garlic-Grilled Eggplant · Jo's Easy Squash
· Ultimate Mashed Potatoes · Cheddar–Baked Potato Slices ·
Mashed Yucca · JR's Barbecued Rice

Man and woman cannot live by meat alone. At times we want vegetables! Whether you are serving barbecue or grilled beef, chicken, or fish, you will want to serve a garden vegetable or potato side dish too. Vegetables are good for you, of course, but equally important, they taste great. Here are some Southern favorites—and a few I included just because I like them.

W'hammed Corn

(thanks to Dr. Richard L. Dixon)

Serves 4 to 5

This recipe is simple and yet will impress your friends—particularly if you decide to divulge the "secret" to its success (the easy recipe!). Credit goes to my inventive dentist friend, who specializes in blowing his guests away with exotic dishes!

2	15-ounce cans whole kernel corn, with the liquid	2	teaspoons Mild Seasoning Mix (page 171) or W'ham Mild Seasoning, or 2 teaspoons salt mixed with 1 teaspoon freshly ground black pepper
4	tablespoons (½ stick) unsalted butter or margarine		

Put the corn and its liquid in a large saucepan. Add the butter and heat over medium-high heat until the butter melts and the liquid comes to a brisk simmer.

Add the seasoning mix and stir well. Reduce the heat to low, cover, and cook for 20 minutes. Remove from the heat, stir, and let stand, covered, for about 10 minutes, or until all the liquid is absorbed, before serving.

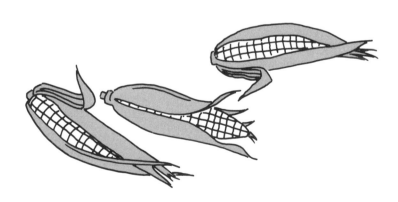

Creamed Fennel
and Corn

(thanks to Nathan Myhrvold)

Fennel is an uncommon vegetable but a wonderful one. It has a crunchy texture and sweet anise (licorice) flavor that goes just great with corn. For this recipe, use summer's sweetest, freshest corn and take great care not to overcook it. Just warm it through.

1	small fennel	1	cup heavy cream
5	ears fresh sweet corn		Salt to taste
3	tablespoons unsalted butter or margarine		Freshly ground black pepper to taste

Trim the feathery fronds from the fennel and cut out the tough root section. Remove and discard any immature fronds inside the bulb. Dice the bulb into pieces the size of corn kernels.

Cut the kernels from the corn and set aside.

In a large frying pan, heat the butter over medium heat until melted. Add the fennel and cook, stirring, for about 10 minutes, or until it is softened and almost translucent. The fennel will resemble onions and its licorice fragrance will fill the kitchen.

Add the cream and cook for 4 to 5 minutes until reduced by half. Reduce the heat to medium-low and add the corn kernels. Cook for 2 to 3 minutes until the corn is heated through. Do not overcook. Season with salt and pepper and serve immediately.

Notes: —*The easiest way to cut the kernels from a corn cob is to stand the cob upright on a cutting board and, using a sharp knife, slice down, cutting the kernels from the cob.*

If you prefer, substitute 1 large sweet onion for the fennel. Use Vidalia, Walla Walla, Texas sweet, or Maui sweet onions.

Grilled Herb-Marinated Vegetables

(thanks to Les Kincaid)

Serves 4 to 6

 Nothing tastes better with grilled meat than grilled vegetables. Serve these hot or at room temperature.

Vinaigrette Marinade

5 tablespoons balsamic vinegar

1 tablespoon Dijon mustard

¼ cup olive oil

3 tablespoons minced fresh thyme

2 teaspoons salt

Freshly ground black pepper to taste

Vegetables

1 medium-sized red onion, cut into ½-inch slices

6 to 7 scallions, trimmed and left whole

3 Asian eggplants, cut in half lengthwise

1 red bell pepper, seeded and quartered

1 green bell pepper, seeded and quartered

2 medium-sized red potatoes, sliced and blanched in boiling water until just fork-tender (optional)

In a small bowl, combine the vinegar and mustard and whisk to blend. Slowly add the oil, whisking constantly, until emulsified. Season with the thyme, salt, and pepper.

Put the vegetables in a large glass or ceramic bowl and toss well. Add the vinaigrette and set aside to marinate for at least 15 minutes and up to 1 hour, stirring several times.

Prepare the grill. Ignite the coals and let them burn until covered with white ash. Spray the grill rack with vegetable spray.

Grill the vegetables for 20 to 30 minutes until tender, turning 1 or 2 times. Serve immediately or at room temperature.

When draining vegetables or pasta, run cold water in the sink. This stops the steam from scalding your hands.

Garlic Grilled Eggplant

(thanks to Charles K. Bowen)

Serves 4

When it's grilled, eggplant makes a great side dish with barbecue—even folks like me, who don't much like it any other way, dig into this garlicky grilled vegetable. With this one preparation the exception, I believe that humankind has no business consuming anything that is dark purple. Try it, you'll like it!

2	medium-to-large eggplants, sliced into ½-inch rounds	¼	cup garlic-flavored olive oil (see the Note)
2	teaspoons salt	½	teaspoon freshly ground black pepper, or more if you prefer

Lay the eggplant slices on a paper towel–lined baking sheet or tray and sprinkle with half the salt. Turn the slices over and salt the other side. Let the eggplant slices sit for about 10 minutes to "sweat." Turn them after 5 minutes.

Prepare the grill. Ignite the coals and let them burn until covered with white ash. Spray the grill rack with vegetable spray.

Pat the eggplant slices dry, removing as much salt as possible, and place them in a shallow baking dish large enough to hold them in a single layer (you may have to use 2 dishes).

Drizzle the eggplant slices with half the oil and half the pepper. Turn them over and drizzle them with the remaining oil and pepper.

Grill the eggplant slices for 20 to 25 minutes, turning them several times, until tender and charred. Serve at once.

Note:—*While you can buy garlic-flavored olive oil in specialty stores and through catalogues, you can also make your own. There are two methods I like. First, the easy way is to warm the olive oil in a small pan and stir in some garlic powder (don't mistakenly use garlic salt!). For ¼ cup of* *oil, you will need 1 teaspoon of garlic powder. Use the oil right away. The second method is to peel 1 or 2 cloves of garlic and drop them into an 8- to 10-ounce bottle of olive oil. Let the oil sit at room temperature for at least 24 hours to infuse it with the garlic—and longer for more intense flavor. When it reaches the desired intensity, strain the oil and use it as directed in the recipe. The garlic oil made by this method will keep in a cool, dark cupboard just as any oil does.*

Jo's Easy Squash

(thanks to Jo Grisham)

Serves 4 to 6

My good friend Jo came up with the easy way to turn canned squash into something memorable.

2	12-ounce cans winter squash	1	teaspoon salt
4	tablespoons (½ stick) butter or margarine	½	teaspoon sugar
3	tablespoons chopped onions		Freshly ground black pepper to taste

In a saucepan, combine the squash, butter, onions, salt, and sugar. Add pepper to taste. Cook over medium-high heat until bubbling. Reduce the heat to low and cook for 10 minutes. Remove from the heat, cover, and let stand for 5 minutes before serving.

A lump of sugar added to water when cooking green vegetables helps them retain their fresh color.

Ultimate
Mashed Potatoes

(thanks to Nathan Myhrvold)

Serves 6

Here is a mashed potato lover's dream—and, guess what? These go great with bar-becue! There's a lot of garlic in the potatoes, but the slow cooking in the cream and butter sweetens the garlic so that the final flavor is rich and mild. Even people who think they don't like garlic will love these potatoes.

1	head of garlic	2
1	shallot, quartered (but not peeled)	
4	to 5 dried shiitake mushrooms or other dried mushrooms	
1½	cups heavy cream	
1	cup (2 sticks) butter, cut into pieces	

1 head of garlic

1 shallot, quartered (but not peeled)

4 to 5 dried shiitake mushrooms or other dried mushrooms

1½ cups heavy cream

1 cup (2 sticks) butter, cut into pieces

2 pounds all-purpose potatoes, peeled and cubed

Salt to taste

Freshly ground white pepper to taste

Remove the papery outer layers from the head of garlic. Using the heel of your hand, press down on the head to separate the cloves. Do not peel the cloves.

In a saucepan, combine the garlic cloves, shallot, mushrooms, cream, and butter. Cook on low heat for 20 to 30 minutes until the garlic cloves are very soft. Check often and add more cream if necessary during cooking.

Strain the cream mixture into another saucepan. Keep the liquid warm by covering the pan and putting it in a warm place. Let the solids cool.

In a large saucepan, cook the potatoes in lightly salted water to cover by about 1 inch over high heat until boiling. Reduce the heat and simmer for about 20 minutes until the potatoes are tender and can easily be pierced with the tip of a knife. Drain and return the potatoes to the pan.

Set the pan over low heat and shake the pan gently for a few minutes to dry the potatoes. Remove from the heat and set aside to cool.

Transfer the cream to a blender or food processor. Using your fingers, squeeze the pulp from each clove of garlic into the cream. Discard the outer skin. Squeeze the shallot pulp into the cream and discard its skin. Put the mushrooms into a small strainer and press against its sides to extract as much liquid as possible from the mushrooms. Add the liquid to the cream. Discard the mushrooms or chop them coarsely and add them to the cream. (They will show up in the potatoes as brown flecks.) Purée the mixture until smooth (if you are using the mushrooms, the mixture will not be completely smooth). Season to taste with salt and pepper.

Mash the potatoes with a potato masher or fork. Add the puréed garlic cream and continue to mash and stir until well mixed and lump-free. Heat over medium heat until hot. Serve at once.

Most of us know how to say nothing.
Few of us know when.

Cheddar–Baked
Potato Slices

(thanks to Darlene Ryan)

Serves 4

 Try this with grilled or broiled meat. Easy and wonderful.

1   8-ounce can cream of mush-room soup

½   teaspoon freshly ground black pepper

½   teaspoon paprika

4   baking potatoes, cut into slices

1   cup shredded Cheddar cheese or American cheese

Preheat the oven to 350°F.

In a small bowl, combine the soup, pepper, and paprika.

Arrange the potatoes in overlapping slices in a rectangular or oblong baking dish. Pour the soup mixture over the slices. Sprinkle the cheese over the top. Cover with foil and bake for 45 minutes. Uncover and bake for about 10 minutes longer, or until the slices are tender and the sauce is bubbling hot. Serve at once.

Mashed Yucca

(thanks to Quint Smith)

Serves 12

 This dish is traditionally served with barbecued kid (goat, that is!). But I find it's tasty with any barbecued meat.

4	pounds yucca, peeled and coarsely chopped	1	cup (2 sticks) butter, cut into pieces
2	cups heavy cream		Salt to taste
			Freshly ground black pepper to taste

In a large saucepan, cover the yucca with lightly salted water. Bring to a boil and cook over medium-high heat for about 20 minutes, or until fork-tender. Drain.

Mash the yucca in a food mill or with a ricer, potato masher, or fork. (Do not use a food processor; the yucca will turn gluelike.) Transfer the yucca to a large bowl.

In a small saucepan, heat the cream and butter until the butter melts and the cream is steaming hot. Pour over the yucca and stir to mix. Season with salt and pepper and serve immediately.

JR's Barbecued Rice

(thanks to J.R. Roach)

Serves 12 to 14

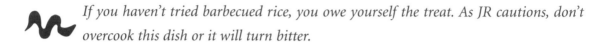 *If you haven't tried barbecued rice, you owe yourself the treat. As JR cautions, don't overcook this dish or it will turn bitter.*

2 tablespoons chicken bouillon granules	¾ teaspoon crushed dried thyme
6 cups hot water	¾ teaspoon garlic powder
2½ cups long grain rice	¼ teaspoon crushed dried rosemary
½ cup chopped celery	¼ teaspoon freshly ground black pepper
⅓ cup chopped green bell pepper	5 to 6 drops Tabasco sauce
¾ cup chopped onions	4 tablespoons (½ stick) butter or margarine
2 tablespoons Worcestershire sauce	

Prepare the cooker (pages 11–13), allowing it to reach a temperature of 250°F.

In a large foil pan, dissolve the bouillon granules in the water. Add the rice, celery, bell pepper, onion, Worcestershire, thyme, garlic powder, rosemary and pepper. Season to taste with Tabasco. Scatter pats of butter over the top and then stir to incorporate.

Cover and cook for about 30 minutes, or until the liquid is absorbed by the rice. Uncover, stir to distribute the vegetables, and cook at 200°F (at the cool end of the cooker) for about 1 hour, stirring occasionally. Do not overcook. Serve immediately.

10

Slaws, Salads, Dressings, and Sandwiches

Simple Coleslaw · Cajun Coleslaw · Brownwood-Style Coleslaw · Creole Cabbage Salad · Texas Steakhouse Salad · Dixie Caesar Salad · Tomato-Onion Salad · Lillie's Chicken Salad · Mustard-Vinegar Dressing · Garden Club Slaw Dressing · Cucumber-Cream Dressing · Moe's Salad Dressing · Mayonnaise · Eggless Mayonnaise · Jubilation Plantation BBQ Sandwich · Smokehouse Dixie Chicken Sandwich · Bologna Sandwich · BLTMOP

Cool, creamy coleslaw is as natural a partner for barbecue as ice is for tea. In some parts of the South, coleslaw is a prerequisite for barbecue. Coleslaw is a modern-day version of the cabbage salads that came to America with Dutch and German settlers, and which became extremely popular in this region. It seems only fitting that Memphis, the buckle of the barbecue belt, is where it all began. In fact, the story goes that the first time coleslaw was served on a barbecue sandwich, was in Memphis. It was used to "stretch" the meat one afternoon at

Leonard's BBQ, when supplies ran low. Need I mention that the combination was an instant success?

Southerners like other salads too, and I have included a few. Any cool, tangy, crunchy salad tastes good with full-flavored, tender barbecue. And both slaws and salads are ideal dishes for backyard parties and other outdoor gatherings, where the main course may be barbecue, something grilled, or perhaps a big pot of chili. For good measure, I have included a few salad and slaw dressings so that you can improvise with your favorite combinations of greens and other raw vegetables.

Slaws and salads go hand in hand with sandwiches—both are quick and suitable for casual get-togethers. Sandwiches made from barbecued pork and Smokehouse Dixie Chicken (page 53) are truly unbelievable—and both call for coleslaw as an ingredient. Finally, I provide you with two outrageous sandwiches—one made with bologna and the other with bacon and peanut butter.

Simple
Coleslaw

(pure Willingham)

Serves 14 to 16;
makes 48 barbecue sandwiches

I recommend this simple slaw on a shredded pork or beef barbecue sandwich. Use about an ounce (2 tablespoons) for each sandwich. Um-umm good! It also makes a tasty side dish.

1 large head green cabbage, cored and shredded (about 3 pounds)	1 tablespoon prepared mustard or Willingham's Old Phartz Mustard
1 small carrot, shredded	1 tablespoon dill pickle juice
1 small sweet onion, such as Vidalia or Walla Walla, diced	1 tablespoon Mild Seasoning Mix (page 171) or W'ham Mild Seasoning
1 cup Garden Club Slaw Dressing (page 144)	

In a bowl, combine the cabbage, carrot, and onion and mix well.

In another bowl, combine the salad dressing, mustard, pickle juice, and seasoning mix. Spoon over the cabbage mixture and toss to mix well. Cover and refrigerate for at least 30 minutes and up to 3 days.

Cajun Coleslaw

(thanks to L. J. Goldstock)

This light and sassy Cajun slaw goes great with grilled chicken, beef tenders, pork chops, or barbecue. The Cajun spices heat it up just enough to give it the zest it needs to perk up plain meat. Here's a tip: To save time and energy, use the food processor to shred the vegetables.

2	tablespoons vegetable oil	⅓	cup packed light brown sugar
1	cup finely chopped onions	1	tablespoon Dijon mustard
⅓	cup diced celery	3	tablespoons cornstarch
⅓	cup shredded carrots	3	tablespoons cider vinegar
1	cup thinly sliced red bell pepper	¼	teaspoon Cajun Seasoning Mix
3	cups shredded green cabbage		(page 172) or W'ham Cajun Hot
1	cup shredded red cabbage		Seasoning or W'ham Hot Stuff
2	cups apple juice		Seasoning

In a large skillet, heat the oil over medium heat. Add the onions, celery, carrots, and bell pepper and cook, stirring, for about 10 minutes until the onions are translucent. Add the cabbages, cover, and cook for about 5 minutes longer just until the cabbage begins to soften.

In a small bowl, combine the apple juice, brown sugar, mustard, cornstarch, vinegar, and seasoning mix. Stir into the warm vegetables and cook for about 10 minutes longer, or until the sauce is thick and clear. Serve warm, at room temperature, or cold.

Note: *The coleslaw keeps in the refrigerator for up to 5 days.*

Brownwood-Style Coleslaw

(thanks to Don Grogg)

Serves 8 to 10

This good-looking fruit- and vegetable-filled coleslaw tastes unbelievable with barbecued ribs, shredded pork, you name it! Always make more than you think you will need because you are sure to eat more than you plan to. Do not let the slaw sit for too long before serving or the apples and avocados may darken. Once it is dressed, the lemon juice will retard this process.

Dressing

1 cup store-bought poppy seed dressing

1 cup freshly squeezed lemon juice or apple cider vinegar

1 teaspoon freshly ground black pepper

1 teaspoon salt

Slaw

1 large head purple or green cabbage, cored, halved, sliced ½ to ¾ inch thick, and chopped

2 cups whole seedless red and green grapes

2 avocados, pitted, peeled, and sliced

2 tart apples, such as Granny Smith, peeled and chopped

¾ cup pecans or walnuts, toasted or not—your choice

5 to 6 green onions (both white and tender green parts), chopped

2 tablespoons chopped cilantro

To make the dressing, whisk the poppy seed dressing with the lemon juice. Season with pepper and salt. Cover and refrigerate for at least 1 hour and up to 6 hours.

To make the slaw, toss the cabbage, grapes, avocados, apples, and pecans in a large glass or ceramic bowl. Pour the dressing over the slaw. Add the green onions and cilantro and mix gently. Serve immediately or cover and refrigerate.

Creole Cabbage Salad

(thanks to Betty Dickinson)

Serves 6 to 8

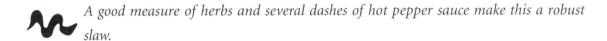 *A good measure of herbs and several dashes of hot pepper sauce make this a robust slaw.*

1	large head green cabbage, shredded	2	teaspoons dried basil
½	cup olive oil	½	teaspoon powdered thyme
2	tablespoons water	3	tablespoons red wine vinegar
1	beef bouillon cube	2	garlic cloves, minced
1	medium-sized onion, finely chopped	½	teaspoon salt
10	shallots, finely chopped	5	to 6 dashes hot pepper sauce or to taste
1	tablespoon minced fresh parsley		Freshly ground black pepper to taste

Put the cabbage in a large bowl and sprinkle with 4 tablespoons of the olive oil. Toss to coat thoroughly and set aside.

In a small saucepan, heat the water over medium heat. Add the bouillon cube and mash it with a spoon or fork. Stir until it's dissolved. Remove from the heat and cool to room temperature. Add to the cabbage.

Add the onion, shallots, parsley, basil, and thyme. Toss to mix.

In a small bowl, whisk together the remaining 4 tablespoons olive oil and the vinegar. Add the garlic and salt and whisk to mix. Season with hot pepper sauce and pepper. Pour over the cabbage and toss to mix. Serve immediately or cover and refrigerate for up to 3 hours.

Texas Steakhouse Salad

(thanks to Don Grogg)

Serves 4 to 6

You guessed it. This is great with big, juicy, Texas-sized steaks. The recipe can be doubled as many times as needed to serve a squad, platoon, company, regiment, battalion, or army. Yours and theirs!

Salad

1 head iceberg lettuce, torn into pieces

1 tomato, peeled, seeded, and coarsely chopped

6 to 7 green onions (both white and tender green parts), chopped

½ cup jalapeño- or pimiento-stuffed green olives, sliced

Dressing

Juice of 1 lemon

4 tablespoons red wine vinegar or balsamic vinegar

2 tablespoons Dijon mustard or Willingham's Old Phartz Mustard

½ cup extra virgin olive oil

½ teaspoon freshly ground black or green pepper

½ teaspoon garlic salt

Garnish

2 avocados, pitted, peeled, and sliced

½ cup chopped cilantro

¼ cup crumbled feta, blue cheese, or sharp Cheddar cheese (about 1 ounce)

continued

To make the salad, toss the lettuce, tomato, green onions, and olives in a glass or ceramic bowl. Cover and refrigerate for at least 1 hour.

To make the dressing, in a small bowl, whisk together the lemon juice, vinegar, and mustard. Slowly add the olive oil, whisking until emulsified. Season to taste with pepper and garlic salt.

Pour the dressing over the salad and toss to coat. Garnish with avocado slices, cilantro, and crumbled cheese. Serve immediately.

Dixie Caesar Salad

(thanks to John P. Young)

Serves 4

 "U ken lie 'bout how u made disun, donchano!" It's so easy, no one will believe the truth!

½ cup olive oil

Dash of red wine vinegar

1 teaspoon Worcestershire sauce

1 garlic clove, crushed

¼ teaspoon dry mustard

1 teaspoon salt

½ teaspoon freshly ground black pepper

1 teaspoon Mild Seasoning Mix (page 171) or W'ham Mild Seasoning

2 anchovy fillets, finely chopped

2 small heads romaine lettuce, tough outer leaves discarded, other leaves washed and torn into pieces

2 large eggs

⅓ cup freshly squeezed lemon juice

¾ cup freshly grated Parmesan cheese

3 to 4 tablespoons store-bought seasoned croutons

In a large salad bowl, whisk together the olive oil, vinegar, Worcestershire sauce, garlic, mustard, salt, pepper and, seasoning mix. Add the anchovies, cover, and let stand for 4 to 6 hours.

Put the romaine in a large ceramic or wooden salad bowl and pour the dressing over it.

Just before serving, whisk together the eggs and lemon juice and pour over the salad. Toss to mix. Sprinkle with the cheese and top with the croutons. Serve immediately.

Tomato-Onion Salad

(thanks to Les Kincaid)

Serves 12

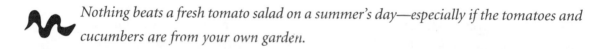 *Nothing beats a fresh tomato salad on a summer's day—especially if the tomatoes and cucumbers are from your own garden.*

⅓	cup white wine vinegar	8	large tomatoes, cored and
½	cup olive oil		quartered
2	teaspoons salt	2	large red onions, thickly sliced
Freshly ground black pepper to taste		3	large cucumbers, peeled, seeded, and chopped

In a bowl, whisk the vinegar and slowly add the olive oil until emulsified. Season with salt and pepper. Cover and refrigerate for at least 2 hours or up to 8 hours.

Put the tomatoes, onions, and cucumbers in a large bowl. Whisk the vinaigrette and pour it over them. Toss gently to mix. Cover and refrigerate for at least 30 minutes. Serve chilled.

Once an onion has been cut in half, rub the cut side with butter to keep it fresh longer.

Lillie's Chicken Salad

(thanks to Lillie Brown)

Serves 4 to 6;

makes 8 to 9 sandwiches

Lillie was the head cook in my first restaurant in Collierville, Tennessee. She sure taught me a lot about the goods and bads of restaurant kitchens. Plus she showed me how to make some great recipes, like this chicken salad, which is one of the all-time great summertime dishes—and this one takes the prize. Serve it over lettuce leaves with fresh fruit, or use it to make chicken salad sandwiches. Outstanding!

1 cup sweet pickle relish	1 tablespoon freshly ground black pepper
2 medium onions, diced	½ teaspoon celery seeds
½ cup chopped celery	4 cups chopped cooked chicken
6 hard-boiled eggs, chopped	white meat (or white and dark
¾ cup Mayonnaise (page 146) or	meat, if preferred)
store-bought mayonnaise	
½ teaspoon salt	

In a medium bowl, combine the relish, onion, celery, and eggs. Stir in the mayonnaise. Add the salt, pepper, and celery seeds. Add the chicken and toss until it is well coated. Cover and refrigerate for at least 1 hour. Let the chicken salad come to room temperature before serving.

Mustard-Vinegar Dressing

(pure Willingham)

Makes about ⅔ cup

This dressing is for salad lovers who find themselves in a restaurant where every dressing on the menu is off their diet. Just ask the waiter for the ingredients and mix up this quickie dressing—it bites back with flavor, not calories, fat, or cholesterol! It's also great at home—mix up a batch and keep it on hand to dress a wedge of lettuce or mixed greens.

6 tablespoons red wine vinegar or cider vinegar	1 teaspoon freshly ground black pepper
2 tablespoons prepared yellow mustard or Willingham's Old Phartz Mustard	1 teaspoon salt (optional)
2 tablespoons corn oil or olive oil	1 tablespoon sugar or granulated artificial sweetener (optional)

In a small bowl, combine the vinegar and mustard. Whisk in the olive oil and season with pepper, salt, and sugar, if using. Use immediately or cover and refrigerate. Whisk before using.

Garden Club
Slaw Dressing

(pure Willingham)

Makes about 2 quarts

Try this on shredded cabbage for coleslaw that is out of this world. I use about one cup for every head of shredded cabbage. Mix the cabbage with shredded carrots and chopped onions if you like. Great! It's a good idea to make this in quantity. You'll want to use it often and it keeps for a couple of weeks in the refrigerator. Let it chill for a good twenty-four hours no matter what—this dressing needs time to rest and steep. Don't we all?

2   quarts store-bought Garden Club salad dressing

½   cup prepared yellow mustard or Willingham's Old Phartz Mustard

4   tablespoons Mild Seasoning Mix (page 171) or W'ham Mild Seasoning

1½ teaspoons Hot Seasoning Mix (page 173) or W'ham Hot Stuff Seasoning

2   tablespoons dill pickle juice

In a large jar or bowl, combine the dressing, mustard, seasoning mixes, and pickle juice. Stir well. Cover and refrigerate for at least 24 hours.

Cucumber–Cream Dressing

(thanks to Steve Uliss)

Makes about 1¼ cups

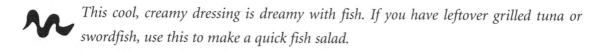 *This cool, creamy dressing is dreamy with fish. If you have leftover grilled tuna or swordfish, use this to make a quick fish salad.*

2   tablespoons freshly squeezed
    lemon juice
1   cup heavy cream, whipped
¼   teaspoon salt

Dash of cayenne pepper
Dash of freshly ground white pepper
¾   cup grated cucumber, well drained

Gently stir the lemon juice into the whipped cream. Add the salt, cayenne, and pepper and then gently fold in the cucumber. Serve immediately

Moe's Salad Dressing

(thanks to Dr. Richard L. Dixon)

Makes about 4½ cups

This is really good over mixed greens and topped with garlic croutons. The recipe makes a lot, so you can use it for a couple of weeks.

continued

2	cups canola oil	1	tablespoon chopped fresh basil
2	cups olive oil	2	tablespoons chopped green onions (both white and tender green parts)
¼	cup ketchup		
4	garlic cloves, crushed		
1	teaspoon seasoned salt	Juice of 1 lime	
½	teaspoon crushed red pepper flakes	Juice of 1 lemon	
		Granulated artificial sweetener	
1	tablespoon chopped fresh oregano		

In a jar or bowl, mix all the ingredients until well blended. Cover and refrigerate for up to 8 hours. Shake or stir well before using.

Mayonnaise

(thanks to Laird Yock)

Makes about 2 ½ cups

 Making mayonnaise is easy once you get the hang of it. The trick is to add the oil very slowly so that it has plenty of opportunity to form an emulsion with the egg yolks.

2	teaspoons salt	2	large egg yolks
1	teaspoon dry mustard or Willingham's Old Phartz Mustard Powder	2	cups olive oil or salad oil
		2	tablespoons cider vinegar
		2	tablespoons tarragon vinegar
Dash of cayenne			

In a glass or ceramic bowl, combine the salt, mustard, and cayenne. Add the egg yolks and whisk vigorously until slightly thickened. Add the oil, drop by drop, whisking continuously. When about half the oil is incorporated, add the rest in a slow, steady stream. Whisk continuously to prevent the mayonnaise from separating.

When the mayonnaise begins to thicken, add the vinegars, a tablespoon at a time, alternating with the oil. Whisk until smooth and blended.

Note: *This is terrific-tasting mayonnaise, but keep in mind that there's always a potential health risk in consuming raw eggs.*

Eggless Mayonnaise

(thanks to Betty Lane)

Makes about 1½ cups

If you're trying to steer clear of eggs, this is the mayo for you. It's homemade and full of flavor and just the right consistency for mixing into salads or spreading on bread. It does not keep, so plan to use it right away.

¼ cup chilled evaporated milk

1 tablespoon white distilled vinegar

1 tablespoon freshly squeezed lemon juice

½ teaspoon salt

½ teaspoon confectioners' sugar

¼ teaspoon dry mustard or Willingham's Old Phartz Mustard Powder

¼ teaspoon paprika

Pinch of Hot Seasoning Mix (page 173) or W'ham Hot Stuff Seasoning, or cayenne pepper

1 cup chilled olive oil or vegetable oil

In a large bowl, combine the evaporated milk, vinegar, lemon juice, salt, confectioners' sugar, mustard, paprika, and seasoning mix. Beat with a rotary egg beater until well blended. Add ⅓ cup of the oil and beat well. Add another ⅓ cup and beat well again. Add the remaining oil and beat until smooth and blended. Serve immediately.

Jubilation Plantation BBQ Sandwich

(thanks to Les Kincaid)

Serves 1

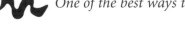 *One of the best ways to eat barbecued pork is as a pulled meat sandwich.*

4   ounces (about ½ cup) Jubilation
    Plantation BBQ (page 62)
¼   cup Creole Cabbage Salad
    (page 138) or other coleslaw
1   hamburger bun

1   recipe Sweet Bar-B-Q Sauce
    (page 158) or W'ham Sweet 'n
    Sassy Sauce, or Hot Bar-B-Q Sauce
    (page 157) or W'ham Hot Sauce,
    for dipping

Spoon the pork onto the bun, top with coleslaw, and serve immediately with barbecue sauce for dipping.

Just ask anyone. At the Willingham's house, putting together pulled and chopped barbecued pork with coleslaw, a dill pickle, and barbecue sauce on a bun is the only way to build a great sandwich. We use a four-inch hamburger bun, about one and a half ounces of pork (or beef), an ounce of coleslaw, two slices of dill pickle, and then just under an ounce (a shy two tablespoons) of W'ham Sweet 'n Sassy Sauce.

If I'm using pork, I use meat from the shoulder or Boston butt—or the meat from a whole hog. With beef, I like brisket or the inside round. What a superb sandwich. I also sometimes mix chopped beef and pork trimmings with some Sweet 'n Sassy Sauce. I call this "pit-blend BBQ" and it's a favorite everywhere I go.

Smokehouse
Dixie Chicken Sandwich

(thanks to Steve Prentiss)

Serves 1

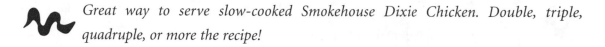 *Great way to serve slow-cooked Smokehouse Dixie Chicken. Double, triple, quadruple, or more the recipe!*

4   ounces (about ½ cup) pulled
     Smokehouse Dixie Chicken meat
     (page 53)
1   hamburger bun

¼   cup Cajun Coleslaw (page 136) or
     other coleslaw
Sweet pickle chips

Spread the chicken in an even layer in a shallow microwave-safe dish. Microwave on high (100 percent) power for 1 minute, or until warm.

Spoon the chicken onto the bun, top with coleslaw and pickle chips, and serve immediately.

Bologna
Sandwich

(pure Willingham)

Serves 1

This sandwich is without question my very—well, almost my very favorite of all my favorite sandwiches. Don't push down on the top of the sandwich once you close it— it will respond much like a greased watermelon: The harder you squeeze the harder it is to hold it in the proper position. Be sure to have lots of napkins, and a bag of potato chips completes the culinary experience. Trust me! Try this mother of all sandwiches!

1 hamburger bun	1 thin slice tomato (about ¼-inch thick)
1 tablespoon Mayonnaise (page 146) or store-bought mayonnaise	
	1 slice onion (about ¼-inch thick)
1 tablespoon creamy peanut butter	1 slice Cheddar cheese or longhorn cheese
2 slices bologna	

Spread one half of the hamburger bun with mayonnaise and the other with peanut butter. Lay a slice of bologna on each. Lay the tomato slice on one side and the onion slice on the other. Lay the cheese over the onion. Close the sandwich and serve immediately.

BLTMOP

(thanks to Marge Willingham)

Serves 1

If you haven't tried this sandwich (and I am pretty sure you have not!), try it, pretty please. Officially, the recipe serves one, but most folks will want at least a sandwich and a half, so plan accordingly.

4	strips bacon	1	tablespoon creamy peanut butter
2	slices white or whole wheat toast	1	large lettuce leaf
1	tablespoon Mayonnaise (page 146)	1	to 2 thick slices onion
	or store-bought mayonnaise	1	to 2 thick slices tomato

Broil, grill, or panfry the bacon until medium crisp (crisp won't work). Drain on paper towels.

Spread one slice of toast with mayonnaise and the other with peanut butter. Place the lettuce on the mayonnaise side and the bacon on the peanut butter side. Top the bacon with the onion slice(s) then with the tomato slice(s). Close the sandwich and serve immediately.

11

Barbecue Sauces, Dry Rubs, Seasoning Mixes, Marinades, Glazes, and Savory Sauces

Mild Bar-B-Q Sauce · Hot Bar-B-Q Sauce · Sweet Bar-B-Q Sauce · Arkansas Country Bar-Be-Que Sauce · Down 'n Dixie Barbecue Sauce · Memphis-Style Bar-B-Q Sauce · Quick Barbecue Sauce · Big Bubba's Bar-B-Q Sauce · Tennessee Home Tomato Sauce · Hurry Yup BBQ Sauce · South Carolina BBQ Sauce · Kansas City–Style Sauce · Mild Seasoning Mix · Cajun Seasoning Mix · Hot Seasoning Mix · General Dry Rub · Cambridge Dry Rub · Beef or Pork Rub · Poultry Rub · Barbecue Dry Rub · All-Purpose Marinade · Cambridge Marinade · Veggie Marinade · Asian-Style Marinade · Beef Marinade · W'ham Hot Wings Sauce · Dip 'em Hot Wings Sauce · Glazes for Baked Ham · Glazes for Roast Leg of Lamb · Bar-B-Q Cocktail Sauce · Horseradish Cocktail Sauce · Tartar Sauce · Chowchow

There's not a barbecue pit master or backyard hobbyist who does not have his or her favorite barbecue sauce. I happen to think my sauces are the best there are. And my dry rubs and marinades, too. All were developed to satisfy my taste buds, and they do that more than any I have ever come across.

I am convinced sauce was invented to cover up mistakes in cooking. The excuses offered for the sauce were to change the overall presentation to accommodate individual taste. Which generally, I suppose, is a good thing. I, however, serve my sauces on the side only. That way, everyone has a choice. Mild, sweet, hot, or hotter! Or, if you like, no sauce at all.

I worked long and hard perfecting the formulas for my sauces, dry rubs, and marinades. When I was satisfied, I put together a business plan to bottle and market them. They're called W'ham products, sold right out of my small office in Memphis. My wife, Marge, and my good friend Jo Grisham work with me (and keep the business running smoothly and efficiently). Many of the recipes call for a specific W'ham sauce, seasoning mix (dry rub), or marinade. If you have the product, great. (There is mail-order information on page 231.) If not, I have provided recipes in this chapter for delicious facsimiles. The recipes throughout the book always offer the options. And if you like food that is so hot it makes you cry, use a hot (Cajun or hot) sauce or dry rub, even if a recipe calls for mild—or vice versa. The heat level is up to the final judge—you!

Sauces and marinades are easy to understand. You generally serve the sauce after the meat is cooked; you soak the meat in the marinade before it is cooked to give it flavor and to tenderize it. But, you may ask, what the heck do you do with a dry rub? A dry rub (also called a seasoning mix, dry spice, or "shake") resembles a marinade more than a sauce. It's a powdery mixture of spices that you rub thoroughly into the meat well before barbecuing or grilling. The rub pulls moisture from the atmosphere and attracts the meat's juices, which rise to the surface and absorb the mingled flavors of the rub. The meat ends up literally marinating in its own juices. These resemble a jelly on the meat's surface, and it's a good idea to rub them back into the meat for greater penetration. If time permits, you will get the best results if you cover and refrigerate the meat overnight after rubbing the meat. This is particularly effective with heavy meats such as brisket, shoulder, and butt.

It's safe to say that about 80 percent of the winners on the barbecue competition circuit use a combination of marinade (or vinegar) and dry rub when preparing their entries. Once you begin using rubs, you'll understand why they work so well and surely will be hooked.

Mild Bar-B-Q Sauce

(pure Willingham)

Makes about 2 quarts

 When you need a good amount of the best-tasting mild barbecue sauce around, try this recipe. Not too hot, not too sweet. I personally recommend it!

4 cups tomato sauce	½ cup Worcestershire sauce
1½ cups cola, such as Coca-Cola or Pepsi or Royal Crown, or beer	2 tablespoons vegetable oil
1½ cups cider vinegar	1 tablespoon soy sauce
1½ cups chili sauce	½ teaspoon Tabasco sauce
¼ cup prepared mustard or Willingham's Old Phartz Mustard	1½ cups packed dark brown sugar
½ cup bottled steak sauce	2 tablespoons freshly ground black pepper
Juice of 2 lemons	2 tablespoons garlic salt
	1 tablespoon dry mustard

In a large saucepan, combine the tomato sauce, cola, vinegar, chili sauce, mustard, steak sauce, lemon juice, Worcestershire sauce, oil, soy sauce, and Tabasco. Stir well. Bring to a simmer over medium heat.

In a small bowl or glass jar with a lid, combine the brown sugar, pepper, garlic salt, and mustard. Stir or shake to blend.

continued

Add the dry ingredients to the tomato mixture and stir well. Increase the heat to medium high and bring to a brisk simmer, stirring frequently. Cook for about 20 minutes or longer for thicker, more intensely flavored sauce. The longer the sauce cooks, the less is its final volume.

Cover the saucepan and reduce the heat to low. Cook for about 30 minutes until the flavors are well blended. Cool to tepid. Use immediately or cover and refrigerate for up to 1 week.

Sauces are generally offered on the side at the table. However, some pit masters will finish the cooking process by cutting the sauce with water, vinegar, wine, beer, oil, or some combination of two or three of these ingredients, and using it to baste the meat just before it is done. Sauces also are added to dressings, gravies, and drinks (try a little hot sauce in a Bloody Mary!).

Hot Bar-B-Q Sauce
(pure Willingham)

Makes about 2 quarts

This is just a variation on the mild barbecue sauce—with a little fire added. Adjust it to your liking.

4   cups tomato sauce

1½ cups cola, such as Coca-Cola or Pepsi or Royal Crown, or beer

1½ cups cider vinegar

1½ cups chili sauce

¼   cup prepared mustard or Willingham's Old Phartz Mustard

½   cup bottled steak sauce

Juice of 2 lemons

½   cup Worcestershire sauce

2   tablespoons vegetable oil

1   tablespoon soy sauce

2   to 3 teaspoons Tabasco sauce or more for hotter, or 1 tablespoon Hot Seasoning Mix (page 173) or W'ham Hot Stuff Seasoning

1¼ cups packed dark brown sugar

2   tablespoons freshly ground black pepper

2   tablespoons garlic salt

1   tablespoon dry mustard

In a large saucepan, combine the tomato sauce, cola, vinegar, chili sauce, mustard, steak sauce, lemon juice, Worcestershire sauce, oil, soy sauce, and Tabasco. Stir well. Bring to a simmer over medium heat.

In a small bowl or glass jar with a lid, combine the brown sugar, pepper, garlic salt, and mustard. Stir or shake to blend.

Add the dry ingredients to the tomato mixture and stir well. Increase the heat to medium-high and bring to a brisk simmer, stirring frequently. Cook for about 20 minutes or longer for thicker, more intensely flavored sauce. The longer the sauce cooks, the less is its final volume.

Cover the saucepan and reduce the heat to low. Cook for about 30 minutes until the flavors are well blended. Cool to tepid. Use immediately or cover and refrigerate for up to 1 week.

Sweet Bar-B-Q Sauce

(pure Willingham)

Makes about 2 quarts

I have sweetened up my basic sauce with a little honey and some butter—you can add or subtract the flavorings to suit your own taste.

4 cups tomato sauce

1½ cups cola, such as Coca-Cola or Pepsi or Royal Crown, or beer

1½ cups cider vinegar

1½ cups chili sauce

¼ cup prepared mustard or Willingham's Old Phartz Mustard

½ cup bottled steak sauce

Juice of 2 lemons

½ cup Worcestershire sauce

2 tablespoons vegetable oil

1 tablespoon soy sauce

1 tablespoon honey

½ teaspoon Tabasco sauce

1½ cups packed dark brown sugar

2 tablespoons freshly ground black pepper

2 tablespoons garlic salt

1 tablespoon butter or margarine

In a large saucepan, combine the tomato sauce, cola, vinegar, chili sauce, mustard, steak sauce, lemon juice, Worcestershire sauce, oil, soy sauce, honey, and Tabasco. Stir well. Bring to a simmer over medium heat.

In a small bowl or glass jar with a lid, combine the brown sugar, pepper, garlic salt, and mustard. Stir or shake to blend.

Add the dry ingredients to the tomato mixture and stir well. Increase the heat to medium high, stir in the butter, and bring to a brisk simmer, stirring frequently. Cook for about 20 minutes or longer for thicker, more intensely flavored sauce. The longer the sauce cooks, the less is its final volume.

Cover the saucepan and reduce the heat to low. Cook for about 30 minutes until the flavors are well blended. Cool to tepid. Use immediately or cover and refrigerate for up to 1 week.

Sauces can make or break a meal of barbecue. I don't cook with sauces but I sure like them handy for slathering on the cooked meat. I use mild, sweet, and hot sauces, according to my state of mind on the particular day. (And if I want to "get even" with someone, I add a little extra heat!)

Depending on where you live, you may prefer a certain type of sauce. Coming from Memphis, I like thick, bold-tasting tomato-based sauces. This wasn't always the case in these parts. Thirty years ago, Memphis was strictly a vinegar-pepper sauce town, but about twenty years ago we witnessed the addition of tomato and brown sugar to some sauces. It crept in slowly but surely, and we have adopted such sauces with gusto—although our tomato-based sauces are more vinegary than others. We like some bite!

In the middle section of South Carolina, they like their sauce made from mustard, while in the eastern part of the state, the barbecue sauces are vinegar- and pepper-based. Farther west, as the state gets mountainous, the sauces begin to include tomatoes and ketchup. North Carolina is justly proud of its famous vinegar- and red pepper–based sauces, which are the only ones sanctioned in the eastern regions of the state. In the Piedmont area of North Carolina, 'cuers prefer what they call Lexington-style sauces, which are also peppery and vinegary, but with a dash of ketchup. Head west toward the Blue Ridge Mountains in North Carolina, and you will find tomato- and brown sugar–based sauces, not too dissimilar from those found in Tennessee. Kansas City folks like thick, sweet red sauces. And in Texas, they often don't use any sauce—they think their barbecue is good enough without it!

Arkansas Country Bar-Be-Que Sauce

(thanks to Dr. James M. Stalker)

Makes about 3 cups

 *This memorable sauce got raves at the July 4 Whole Hog Barbecue.*

1 cup ketchup	1 tablespoon garlic powder
½ cup cider vinegar	1 teaspoon cayenne pepper
¼ cup sugar or honey	1 teaspoon salt
3 tablespoons freshly squeezed lemon juice	1 teaspoon Accent or other flavor enhancer (optional)
1 tablespoon prepared mustard	1 teaspoon store-bought salt-free seasoning mix
1 tablespoon Worcestershire sauce	
2 teaspoons soy sauce	1 teaspoon ground cumin
1 tablespoon lemon pepper or freshly ground black pepper	½ teaspoon dry mustard
	½ to ⅔ cup bourbon

In a large saucepan, combine the ketchup, vinegar, honey, lemon juice, prepared mustard, Worcestershire sauce, and soy sauce. Bring to a simmer over medium-high heat.

In a small bowl or glass jar with a lid, combine the lemon pepper, garlic powder, cayenne, salt, Accent, seasoning mix, cumin, and dry mustard. Stir or shake to blend.

Add a third of the dry ingredients to the sauce. Stir and simmer for 2 to 3 minutes. Add another third, stir and simmer for 2 to 3 minutes. Add the remaining third, stir and simmer for about 20 minutes.

Add the bourbon and stir well. Reduce the heat to low, cover, and cook for 1 hour until the flavors are blended and the sauce is thick. Use immediately or cool to room temperature, cover, and refrigerate for up to 1 week.

Down 'n Dixie
Barbecue Sauce

(thanks to Don Grogg)

Makes about 4 cups

This meat-based barbecue sauce is good as can be with grilled or slow-cooked meat or poultry. It keeps for a couple of weeks and during that time must be protected from kitchen poachers!

⅓ cup beef brisket trimmings, thinly sliced

1 white or yellow medium-sized onion, roughly chopped

2 tablespoons olive oil

2 to 3 green onions (both white and tender green parts), chopped

1½ teaspoons minced garlic

3 cups ketchup

¼ cup honey

Juice of 1 lime

1 jalapeño chile, seeded and chopped

2 tablespoons chopped fresh parsley or 2 teaspoons dried parsley

1 tablespoon Dijon mustard

1½ teaspoons Mild Seasoning Mix (page 171) or W'ham Mild Seasoning

2 to 3 tablespoons cornstarch

2 tablespoons sour mash bourbon

continued

In a food processor fitted with a metal blade, process the brisket and white onion until finely chopped. Alternatively, using a large knife, chop the meat and white onion as fine as possible.

In a large stockpot, heat the olive oil over medium heat. Add the green onions and garlic and cook for about 5 minutes, until the green onions are soft. Add the mixed trimmings and white onion and cook for about 30 minutes, or until the onion is soft and the meat is cooked.

Add the ketchup, honey, lime juice, jalapeño, parsley, mustard, and seasoning mix and bring to a simmer over medium-high heat. Reduce the heat to medium low and cook for about 20 minutes.

Stir 2 tablespoons of cornstarch into ¼ cup warm water until dissolved. (If you like thick sauce, use 3 tablespoons of cornstarch.)

Raise the heat to high and bring the mixture to a boil. Stir in the cornstarch mixture. Reduce the heat to medium high and cook, stirring, for 5 to 6 minutes until the sauce is thick. If you desire, add more cornstarch dissolved in water to thicken the sauce further. Add the bourbon, stir, and serve immediately or cool to room temperature and transfer to a glass or ceramic container. Cover and refrigerate for up to 2 weeks. Reheat before serving.

There is a bigger fool than the one who knows it all—
the person who will argue with him.

Memphis-Style Bar-B-Q Sauce

(thanks to Keith Doane)

Makes about 2 quarts

Keith Doane and Bob Sossaman claim to have a perfect win-loss record in BBQ! They accompanied me to Kansas City for the American Royal and came away with three "Firsts" and a Grand Championship. They announced their retirement to ensure their perfect record. Or so they say. I think it's because I worked them so hard! This sauce from my good buddy Keith is a great finishing sauce for grilled food or as a dip at the table. If you want more sauce, double or triple the ingredients.

5	cups tomato sauce	2	tablespooons plus 1 teaspoon salt
¾	cup yellow hot dog mustard	2	tablespoons plus 1 teaspoon
¾	cup red wine vinegar		freshly ground black pepper
⅓	cup chopped onions	2	teaspoons celery powder
⅓	cup chopped green bell peppers	2	teaspoons onion powder
⅓	cup water	2	teaspoons garlic powder
1	pound dark brown sugar	1	teaspoon paprika

In a large saucepan or Dutch oven, combine the tomato sauce, mustard, and vinegar and bring to a simmer over medium heat. Do not boil.

In a blender or food processor fitted with a metal blade, purée the onions and peppers in the water. Transfer to a small saucepan, bring to a simmer, and cook over medium-high heat for 2 to 3 minutes. Add to the tomato sauce mixture and stir to blend. Continue to simmer the mixture.

In a bowl, combine the brown sugar, salt, pepper, celery powder, onion powder, garlic powder, and paprika. Mix thoroughly. Add a quarter of the dry ingredients to the pan. Stir and simmer for 15 minutes. Add another quarter of the dry ingredients, stir and simmer for 15 minutes. Continue in this manner until all the dry ingredients are incorporated and the mixture is simmering briskly but not boiling.

Cover and reduce the heat to low. Cook for 30 minutes until the sauce thickens and the flavors blend. Serve tepid or at room temperature or transfer to a glass container, cover, and refrigerate for up to 1 week.

Barbecue sauces are taking over the
commerical marketplace and Americans spend in excess of
$480 million a year on these sauces. Kraft General Foods
sells half the sauces made in the United States,
but the most significant growth is in another corner of the
market. Cook-off champs and BBQ restaurants are
bottling their own creations. It's no surprise
that every authentic barbecue cook thinks
his or her sauce is "the best."
And why not? It is!

Quick Barbecue Sauce

(thanks to Birgit Andes)

Makes about 1½ cups

Make this when you need a tasty sauce in a flash. It's good for slathering on grilled chicken or pork or to serve at the table. Birgit cooks with me every year in the Kansas City's American Royal, along with her daughter, Stephanie, and son, Matt.

1 14-ounce bottle ketchup	¼ teaspoon onion salt
1½ tablespoons prepared mustard	½ teaspoon celery seed
1½ tablespoons Worcestershire sauce	⅛ teaspoon liquid smoke
1½ teaspoons freshly squeezed lemon juice	⅛ teaspoon garlic juice
	Tabasco sauce to taste

In a saucepan, combine all the ingredients except the Tabasco. Bring to a simmer over low heat and cook for 10 minutes. Season with Tabasco and continue cooking for 5 to 6 minutes longer. Cool to room temperature. Use immediately or transfer to a glass container, cover, and refrigerate for up to 1 week.

Big Bubba's
Bar-B-Q Sauce

(thanks to Marshall Burgess)

Makes about 4 cups

Marshall has been cooking with me since 1990, although he's been cooking most of his life. He's very serious about barbecue—and it's a great pleasure for me to watch him now teach newcomers and make presentations to the judges. This sauce won first place at the 1990 Rootin' on the River BBQ Contest in Memphis, Tennessee. You can't get much more authentic than that!

1	cup sugar	2	tablespoons freshly ground black pepper
4	tablespoons chili powder		
2	tablespoons salt	2½	cups vinegar
2	teaspoons dry mustard		Juice from 2 lemons
2	tablespoons cayenne pepper	1½	cups tomato paste

In a bowl or glass jar with a lid, combine the sugar, chili powder, salt, mustard, cayenne, and black pepper. Stir or shake to mix.

In a saucepan, combine the vinegar, lemon juice, and tomato paste and bring to a simmer over medium heat.

Add a third of the dry ingredients to the pan. Stir and simmer for 15 minutes. Add a quarter of the remaining dry ingredients, stir, and simmer for 3 to 4 minutes. Add about a third of the remaining dry ingredients, stir and simmer for 3 to 4 minutes. Add the remaining dry ingredients, stir, and raise the heat to medium-high. Bring the mixture to a boil and cook for 4 to 5 minutes, or until thick. Serve tepid or at room temperature or transfer to a glass container, cover, and refrigerate for up to 1 week.

Tennessee Home Tomato Sauce

(pure Willingham)

Makes about 4½ cups

This tomato-based barbecue sauce may be used directly on beef or pork chops or cutlets. It also makes a terrific finishing sauce on grilled poultry or vegetables. Or, use it as the base for your oven BBQ creations.

2 16-ounce cans tomatoes with their juice or 2 pounds fresh tomatoes, chopped, plus 1 cup water	1 medium red bell pepper, seeded and chopped
½ cup beef or pork pan drippings or beef broth	1 sweet onion, such as Vidalia or Walla Walla, chopped
2 tablespoons Mild Seasoning Mix (page 171) or W'ham Mild Seasoning	1 garlic clove, crushed
	1 tablespoon cornstarch (optional)

Strain the tomatoes and their juice through a sieve into a saucepan. If using fresh tomatoes, press them through the strainer and add the water to the saucepan. Reserve the tomato solids. Bring to a simmer over medium heat and cook for 5 minutes.

Add the drippings and seasoning mix. Stir and simmer for 3 to 4 minutes.

In a blender or food processor fitted with a metal blade, purée the pepper, onion, garlic, and tomato solids. Transfer to the tomato mixture, cover, and simmer for about 30 minutes until thick. For thicker sauce, sift the cornstarch over the surface and gently stir into the sauce. Use immediately or cool to room temperature, cover, and refrigerate for up to 1 week.

Hurry Yup BBQ Sauce

(thanks to Frank Simonetti)

Makes about 2 cups

Frank is a giant of a man—in stature, generosity, and kindness. We don't agree on everything, but one thing we do agree on is how special barbecue is as a way to bring folks together for fun, food, and friendship. Frank concocted this recipe to go with his ribs (page 82). It's great on the ribs but good any time you need a sauce in a hurry.

1	cup ketchup	¼	cup chopped onion
½	cup Worcestershire sauce	½	teaspoon coarsely ground black
¼	cup freshly squeezed lemon juice		pepper
¼	cup firmly packed light brown sugar	¼	teaspoon cayenne pepper
		¼	teaspoon salt

In a saucepan, combine all the ingredients. Bring to a simmer over medium heat and cook for about 5 minutes. Use immediately or cool to room temperature, cover, and refrigerate for up to 1 week.

South Carolina BBQ Sauce

(thanks to Les Kincaid)

Makes about 2 cups

Different styles of sauce are found in different regions of the South. For some reason, vinegar-based sauces are the only sort many true-blue sons of the Carolinas will tolerate on barbecued pork (the only meat worth barbecuing, according to regional tradition).

2 cups cider vinegar	1 tablespoon vegetable oil
1 tablespoon freshly ground black pepper	1 tablespoon Worcestershire sauce
1 tablespoon cayenne pepper	1 teaspoon kosher salt
	Hot pepper sauce to taste

In a glass or ceramic bowl, combine the vinegar, black pepper, cayenne oil, Worcestershire sauce, and salt. Season with hot sauce. Set aside at room temperature for about 1 hour to give the flavors time to blend. Use immediately or cool to room temperature, cover, and refrigerate for up to 1 week.

Kansas City–Style Sauce

(thanks to Paul Kirk)

Makes about 4½ cups

Kansas City makes a convincing claim to being the barbecue sauce capital of the world. Not only is its American Royal barbecue contest the largest sauce competition going, it's home to a best-selling national brand called K. C. Masterpiece. Paul Kirk, who bills himself as "the Kansas City Baron of Barbecue," sends this recipe for the thick, sweet sauce that's become identified with his city. Plus, he works tirelessly to support the contest.

¾ cup packed light brown sugar

1 1¼-ounce package regular-flavor chili seasoning

2 teaspoons dry mustard

1 teaspoon ground ginger

½ teaspoon ground allspice

¼ teaspoon cayenne pepper

¼ teaspoon ground mace

¼ teaspoon freshly ground black pepper

1 cup white distilled vinegar

¼ cup molasses

¼ cup water

1 to 3 teaspoons liquid smoke (optional)

1 32-ounce bottle ketchup

In a large saucepan, combine the brown sugar, chili seasoning, mustard, ginger, allspice, cayenne, mace, and black pepper. Add the vinegar, molasses, water, and liquid smoke, if using. Stir until dry ingredients are dissolved. Add the ketchup and stir to mix.

Bring to a boil over high heat, stirring constantly to avoid spattering. Reduce the heat to low, cover, and simmer for 30 minutes. Remove from the heat and let cool to room temperature. Use immediately or cool to room temperature, cover, and refrigerate for up to 1 week.

Mild Seasoning Mix

(pure Willingham)

Makes about ¼ cup

~ *You might want to keep this on hand in larger quantities. Double or triple the recipe according to your needs. Use it as directed in recipes throughout the book and to season salad dressings, sauces, gravies, vegetables, chilis, stews, and on and on.*

2   tablespoons salt
1   teaspoon freshly ground black pepper
1   teaspoon lemon pepper
1   teaspoon cayenne pepper
1   teaspoon chili powder
1   teaspoon dry mustard or Willingham's Old Phartz Mustard Powder

1   teaspoon dark or light brown sugar
½   teaspoon garlic powder
Pinch of cinnamon
Pinch of Accent or other flavor enhancer (optional)

In a small bowl or glass jar with a lid, combine all the ingredients. Stir or shake to mix. Use immediately or store in a cool, dark place for several months.

Here's a good way to use a dry rub (seasoning mix): Lay a sheet of plastic wrap on the countertop and then put the meat on it. Rub the meat thoroughly with the mix, and when you're finished, simply wrap the plastic around the meat. Wrap a second sheet around the meat and refrigerate it for as long as the recipe instructs. It will marinate in its own juices wrapped tight in the plastic.

Cajun Seasoning Mix

(pure Willingham)

Makes about ¼ cup

This is a fiery version of the mild seasoning mix. I added a little more cayenne and chili powder.

2   tablespoons salt

1   teaspoon freshly ground black pepper

1   teaspoon lemon pepper

1½ teaspoons cayenne pepper

1½ teaspoons chili powder

1   teaspoon dry mustard or Willingham's Old Phartz Mustard Powder

1   teaspoon dark or light brown sugar

½   teaspoon garlic powder

Pinch of cinnamon

Pinch of Acćent or other flavor enhancer (optional)

In a small bowl or glass jar with a lid, combine all the ingredients. Stir or shake to mix. Use immediately or store in a cool, dark place for several months.

Hot Seasoning Mix

(pure Willingham)

Makes about ⅓ cup

When I market my hot seasoning mix for retail distribution, I call it "for big kids only." (I do the same with my hot barbecue sauce.) There's good reason for the caveat. This is really hot!

4 tablespoons cayenne pepper	½ teaspoon dry mustard or Willingham's Old Phartz Mustard Powder
1 tablespoon chili powder	
1 tablespoon salt	
1 teaspoon dark or light brown sugar	½ teaspoon white pepper
	½ teaspoon lemon pepper
½ teaspoon freshly ground black pepper	Pinch of MSG (optional)

In a bowl, combine the cayenne, chili powder, and salt. Mix thoroughly.

In another bowl, mix the brown sugar, black pepper, mustard, white pepper, lemon pepper, and MSG, if using. Blend thoroughly. Transfer this mixture to the first bowl and stir to mix. Use immediately or store in a cool dark place for several months.

During cooking, meat releases a protein that seals the meat. Most dry rubs contain brown or white sugar and salt, which stimulate the release of the same protein. After it's rubbed, the surface of the meat becomes wet and tacky and, during cooking, in effect produces a new skin. What happens is this: Contrary to what we have been taught all our lives, cold goes to heat. The internal cold of the meat comes through to the outside and gives itself up to the heated atmosphere, corresponding with the temperature of the environment. The cooking environment absorbs the cold and replaces it with heat, all the way to the bone, which is a thermal wick, or through the muscle. To make sure this happens, after rubbing with dry rub, let the meat marinate in its own juices.

Every type of meat requires a different amount of time for this natural marinating to gain the best flavor. Dry rubs generally are used as precooking rubs and may be left on the meat for as long as thirty-six hours or for as short as twenty minutes before the meat is cooked. Additionally, dry rubs (or seasoning mixes) are used as spices in dressings, gravies, sauces, drinks, and even at times are passed at the table for sprinkling on food as individual taste dictates.

CHOPS AND STEAKS —marinate, loosely covered, in juices produced by the dry rub until the meat reaches room temperature.

RIBS —marinate in juices produced by the dry rub overnight (in refrigerator and loosely covered).

POULTRY —marinate in juices produced by the dry rub overnight (in refrigerator and loosely covered).

General Dry Rub

(pure Willingham)

Makes about ¾ cup

 Use this on pork or beef. It's good for poultry too (I prefer the variation for chicken described below) and Cornish game hens, turkey, and game birds.

3	tablespoons salt	1½	teaspoons garlic salt
2	tablespoons dark or light brown sugar	1	teaspoon white pepper
1	tablespoon freshly ground black pepper	1	teaspoon chili powder
1	tablespoon powdered citric acid	½	teaspoon onion salt
1½	teaspoons lemon pepper	½	teaspoon dry mustard or Willingham's Old Phartz Mustard Powder

In a small bowl or glass jar with a lid, combine all the ingredients. Stir or shake to mix. Use immediately or store in a cool, dark place for several months.

Variations: *For chicken, add ½ to ¾ teaspoon of dried coriander (not coriander seeds).*

For lamb, add 1 tablespoon crushed or pulverized fresh mint leaves or 1 teaspoon dried mint, ½ teaspoon cumin, and ½ teaspoon dried coriander.

Cambridge Dry Rub

(thanks to Chris Schlesinger)

Makes about 1 cup

I adapted this rub from a recipe by my good friend Chris Schlesinger. His version is in his book The Thrill of the Grill, *which he wrote with John Willoughby. I have altered the quantities of the ingredients to suit my own tastes. This is an excellent all-purpose rub for chicken, fish, pork, beef, or lamb, and can also be a breading for deep-frying. Sprinkle it into the batter for deep-fried zucchini, onion rings, or mushrooms. Wow! For a basting sauce or marinade, I add soy sauce, vinegar, and water (see Cambridge Marinade, page 183).*

¼ cup dark or light brown sugar

2 tablespoons plus 1½ teaspoons salt

2 tablespoons plus 1½ teaspoons freshly ground black pepper

2 tablespoons plus 1½ teaspoons chili powder

1 tablespoon plus 1½ teaspoons cumin

1 tablespoon plus 1½ teaspoons paprika

1 teaspoon garlic powder (optional)

1 teaspoon lemon pepper (optional)

In the top half of a double boiler set over simmering water, combine all the ingredients. Cook for about 20 minutes, stirring every 5 minutes or so, until the sugar begins to melt and the mixture thickens. Remove from the heat and let the mixture cool to 100°F.

Pass the mixture through a sifter. Use immediately or store in a cool, dark place for several months.

Beef
or Pork Rub

(pure Willingham)

Makes about 1 cup

With this rub you have enough good stuff to add great flavor to fifteen pounds of spareribs, two pounds of back ribs, two fifteen-pound shoulders, a five- to six-pound pork butt, or a dozen individual beef steaks. Wow! Well worth the effort to make up a batch and have it on hand. The cornstarch prevents caking.

4　tablespoons salt
3　tablespoons packed dark brown
　　sugar
1　tablespoon onion salt
1　tablespoon freshly ground black
　　pepper
1　tablespoon white pepper

1　tablespoon lemon pepper
1　tablespoon cayenne pepper
1　tablespoon chili powder
1　tablespoon dried thyme
1　tablespoon dried rosemary
1　tablespoon cornstarch

In the top of a double boiler, combine all the ingredients except the cornstarch. Heat over simmering water until the ingredients are warm to the touch (about 160°F). Stir continuously during heating. As the sugar dissolves, it may form a crust.

Transfer to a bowl and cool to room temperature. Break apart the crust and rub the mixture between your fingers so that it returns to granular form. Add the cornstarch and stir. Use immediately or store in a tightly covered glass container in a cool, dark place for several months.

Poultry Rub

(pure Willingham)

Makes about 1 cup

You can make this rub ahead of time and use it on chicken, turkey, quail, duck, dove, pheasant, goose—you name it. Just use your imagination and surprise your friends with a "from-scratch" rub for grilled fowl. The cornstarch prevents caking and there's enough rub here to rub the insides and outsides of fifteen pounds of split chicken or forty-four pounds of turkey (that's two twenty-two-pound birds!).

4	tablespoons salt	1	tablespoon lemon pepper
3	tablespoons light brown sugar	1	tablespoon cayenne pepper
1	tablespoon onion salt	1	tablespoon chili powder
1	tablespoon freshly ground black pepper	1	tablespoon dried marjoram
		1	tablespoon dried sage
1	tablespoon white pepper	1	tablespoon cornstarch

In the top of a double boiler, combine all the ingredients except the cornstarch. Heat over simmering water until the ingredients are warm to the touch (about 160°F). Stir continuously during heating. As the sugar dissolves, it may form a crust.

Transfer to a bowl and cool to room temperature. Break the crust and rub the mixture between your fingers so that it returns to granular form. Add the cornstarch and stir. Use immediately or store in a tightly covered glass container in a cool, dark place for several months.

Barbecue Dry Rub

(thanks to Dr. James M. Stalker)

Makes about 1½ cups

This rub is pretty strong and so I do not recommend it for thin cuts (like ribs). But it is swell on heavier cuts of meat such as beef round, prime rib, pork shoulder, and even the whole hog. With this recipe, you have enough for five shoulders or four hams. Best if you let the meat marinate, loosely covered, in the refrigerator for a good twenty-four to forty-eight hours after being rubbed.

4 tablespoons ground cumin	2 tablespoons salt
4 tablespoons dried thyme	2 tablespoons curry powder
4 tablespoons garlic powder	1 tablespoon onion powder
4 tablespoons freshly ground black pepper	1 tablespoon Accent or other flavor enhancer (optional)
2 tablespoons cayenne pepper	

In a small bowl or glass jar with a lid, combine all the ingredients. Stir or shake to mix. Use immediately or store in a cool, dark place for several months.

Marinades are used to cleanse and open the pores in the meat so that it can receive the flavorings in the marinade and the dry rub.

Marinades are used to baste meat during cooking. Basting mixtures rarely contain tomatoes, brown sugar, or molasses, which means that tomato-based barbecue sauces are not basting sauces.

After the meat is cooked, I often mix the marinade with the meat drippings and use it to brush on pulled or shredded meat. This is called a back basting.

Finishing sauces may be marinades or barbecue sauces. They are brushed on the meat right at the end of cooking.

Marinades that have been boiled so that they thicken a little, as well as barbecue sauces, are called dipping, brush-on, or spreading sauces. These are served with the cooked meat.

A note of caution: It's important to boil any marinade that has been in contact with raw meat, poultry, fish, or seafood before using it as a finishing or dipping sauce.

All-Purpose Marinade

(pure Willingham)

Makes about 2 cups

Use this to marinate meat, poultry, and vegetables. Or use it to baste, back-baste (page 180), or as a dip. It's also tasty added to Bloody Marys, Virgin Marys, and bullshots. And it's great in salad dressings.

1 cup cider vinegar	1 tablespoon lemon pepper
½ cup freshly squeezed orange juice, unstrained	1 tablespoon freshly ground black pepper
½ cup freshly squeezed lemon juice	1 teaspoon Tabasco sauce or other hot pepper sauce
2 to 3 thin slices lemon peel	½ teaspoon garlic powder
1 tablespoon packed dark brown sugar	

In a glass or ceramic bowl, combine all the ingredients. Use immediately or cover and refrigerate for up to 24 hours.

Don't be afraid of opposition. Remember, a kite rises against the wind, not with it.

I started developing a basic recipe for a marinade when I lived in Washington, D.C., in the early 1970s and first tasted the marinade used at Trader Vic's restaurant. I was dining there with my friends Rose and Lee Elder (yes, the same Lee Elder, the professional golfer!) and was intrigued by the flavor of the meat. Our waiter, a fellow known as Little Pete, was mum on the formula, no matter how much I cajoled.

I went home and worked on my own version. When I was satisfied, I poured it into a peanut butter jar and carried it into the restaurant. Guess what? Little Pete and everyone else was amazed at how good it was—and how close to their own carefully guarded secret. Trader Vic himself tasted the marinade and confessed that if he didn't already have one, he'd buy mine! He gave me five autographed copies of his books, which I treasure to this day. When I examined the autographs, I realized his real name was Victor J. Bergernon.

As a footnote to the story, I was in Washington in the spring of 1995 and ate at Trader Vic's. The manager, Hank Lee, recognized me and, unbeknownst to me, put in a call to Rose Elder. She made her way directly to the restaurant and we had a warm and happy reunion.

Cambridge Marinade

(thanks to Chris Schlesinger)

Makes about 2½ cups

Use this marinade for chicken or meat—good, good, good! It's one of Chris Schlesinger's formulas, who is a devoted student in the art of barbecue and a true master of the grill.

1	cup soy sauce	½	cup water
1	cup apple cider vinegar	1	cup Cambridge Dry Rub (page 176)

In a bowl, combine the soy sauce, vinegar, and water. Add the dry rub and mix until dissolved. Use immediately or cover and refrigerate for up to 24 hours.

Veggie Marinade

(thanks to Birgit Andes)

Makes about 1 cup

Use this marinade for vegetables you plan to roast, stir-fry, or grill directly on the grid or threaded on a skewer. Use this on vegetables such as carrots, mushrooms, zucchini, yellow squash, and parboiled new potatoes. For best results, spread the veggies in a shallow dish, pour over the marinade, and marinate in the refrigerator for at least three hours (two to three hours longer is better).

continued

¾	cup olive oil	½	teaspoon salt
½	cup dry white wine	½	teaspoon freshly ground black
4	garlic cloves, pressed		pepper
2	tablespoons Italian seasoning		

In a glass or ceramic bowl, combine all the ingredients. Stir and use immediately or cover and refrigerate until ready to use.

Asian-Style Marinade

(thanks to Birgit Andes)

Makes about ¾ cup

 Really good for beef and pork, this marinade is equally delicious for chicken. Let the meat marinate for at least three hours, covered, in the fridge.

½	cup soy sauce	2	tablespoons packed dark brown
1	tablespoon Worcestershire sauce		sugar
¼	cup sherry	2	slices fresh ginger
2	garlic cloves, crushed		

In a glass or ceramic bowl, combine all the ingredients. Stir and use immediately or cover and refrigerate until ready to use.

Beef Marinade

(thanks to Birgit Andes)

Makes about 1 ¼ cups

 This is a classic for beef destined for the grill. You can substitute vegetable oil for the olive oil or use a combination of half and half.

1	cup olive oil
¼	cup sugar
2	tablespoons soy sauce
4	tablespoons finely chopped green onions (both white and tender green parts)

2	garlic cloves, minced
½	teaspoon salt
½	teaspoon freshly ground black pepper

In a large bowl, combine all the ingredients. Stir and use immediately or cover and refrigerate until ready to use.

I use large plastic garbage bags to line my coolers and keep them clean. I put marinated ribs in garbage bags inside the coolers. When I do this, I double-bag them so that the sharp points of the bones don't puncture the bags. I put marinated whole tenderloins and other cuts of meat in garbage bags too.

W'ham Hot Wings Sauce

(pure Willingham)

Makes about 4½ cups

Are you ready for this sauce for hot wings? If you add the hot seasoning mix, the sauce will light up your life—and anyone standing near you too! Use it with the hot wings on page 21.

2   cups (4 sticks) butter or margarine

1   cup Mild Seasoning Mix (page 171) or W'ham Mild Seasoning

1   cup All-Purpose Marinade (page 181) or W'ham Marinade

1   cup red wine vinegar

Pinch of Hot Seasoning Mix (page 173) or W'ham Hot Stuff Seasoning (optional)

In a saucepan, combine the butter, seasoning mix, marinade, and vinegar. Cook over medium-high heat, stirring, until the butter melts and the mixture simmers. Add the hot seasoning mix, if desired. Reduce the heat to medium low and simmer gently for 20 minutes. Cool to tepid.

Transfer to a glass or ceramic container, cover, and refrigerate for at least 24 hours. Serve at room temperature or warmed.

Note: *Another way to use this sauce is to heat it in a large saucepan over medium-high heat until simmering. Put the cooked wings (page 21) in a vegetable basket and submerge the basket in the sauce. Simmer for 4 to 5 minutes. Lift the basket from the sauce, shake off the excess and serve.*

Dip 'em Hot Wings Sauce

(thanks to Jim "Trim" Tabb)

Makes about 1 cup

Use these for the Grilled Hot Wings on page 21, or for just about anything else. Says Jim: "Matter o' fact, you ken make most anything better by dippin' it in this magical sauce." I agree!

1	6-ounce jar apricot preserves	1	teaspoon garlic powder
¼	cup Dijon mustard or Willingham's Oil Phartz Mustard	1	teaspoon fenugreek
¼	cup soy sauce	½	teaspoon chili powder
			Dash of ground cinnamon

In a saucepan, combine all the ingredients. Stir well. Bring to a simmer over medium-high heat. Cook for 4 to 5 minutes, stirring, until smooth. Use immediately or cover and refrigerate for up to 1 week.

Glazes for Baked Ham

(pure Willingham)

Any of the following glazes works great with ham. Bake the ham following your favorite recipe for a precooked, smoked ham and then brush the glaze over the meat about 45 minutes before the ham is done and continue baking until the glaze browns and the sugar, honey, or syrup caramelizes. Each glaze recipe makes about 1 generous cup, enough for a fourteen-pound ham.

Brown Sugar Glaze for Ham

1   cup dark brown sugar
Juice of 1 orange

Rind of 1 orange, coarsely chopped

Heat the brown sugar and orange juice in a saucepan set over medium-high heat. Stir until the sugar melts. Add the orange rind and cook for 2 to 3 minutes longer. Use tepid or at room temperature.

Apple Cider Glaze for Ham

½   cup pure maple syrup
½   cup apple cider or apple juice

2   tablespoons prepared mustard

Heat the maple syrup and apple cider in a saucepan set over medium-high heat. Stir until hot. Add the mustard and cook for 2 to 3 minutes longer, stirring to incorporate the mustard. Use tepid or at room temperature.

Cranberry Glaze for Ham

2   cups fresh cranberries   1   cup pure maple syrup

Heat the cranberries and maple syrup in a saucepan set over medium-high heat for about 5 minutes, or until the berries' skins pop open.

Strain through a fine sieve, pressing on the solids to extract as much liquid as possible. Discard the solids. Use tepid or at room temperature.

Current Glaze for Ham

1   cup currant jelly

Heat the jelly in a saucepan set over medium-high heat, stirring until it liquefies. Use warm or tepid.

Mustard Glaze for Ham

1   cup dark brown sugar   1   tablespoon prepared mustard

Heat the brown sugar and mustard in a saucepan over medium-high heat, stirring, until the sugar melts and the mixture is smooth. Use tepid or warm.

Orange Glaze for Ham

1   cup orange marmalade

Heat the marmalade in a saucepan over medium-high heat, stirring, until it liquefies. Use warm or tepid.

Pineapple-Honey Glaze for Ham

¾   cup unsweetened pineapple juice   ½   teaspoon prepared mustard
¾   cup honey

Heat the pineapple juice and honey in a saucepan over medium-high heat, stirring until the honey liquefies. Stir in the mustard and cook for about 5 minutes longer, or until the glaze thickens slightly. Use tepid or warm.

Glazes for Roast Leg of Lamb
(pure Willingham)

Any of the following glazes works great with a leg of lamb. Roast the lamb following your favorite recipe. Use the glazes as instructed in the individual recipes. Each glaze recipe makes about 1 cup, enough for a six- to eight-pound leg of lamb.

Apricot Glaze for Lamb

2   cups canned apricots with the   ¾   cup sugar
    juice

Strain the apricots and juice through a sieve into a small saucepan, pressing on the fruit to extract as much liquid as possible. Heat over medium heat until warm. Add the sugar and cook, stirring, until the sugar dissolves and the glaze thickens. Cool to tepid and brush the lamb frequently during roasting.

Grape Glaze for Lamb

½ cup chopped fresh mint leaves   ½ cup water
½ cup grape jelly

Before roasting, rub the mint leaves into the lamb. Roast the lamb as instructed in your favorite recipe.

In a small saucepan, combine the jelly and water and cook over medium heat for about 5 minutes, or until the jelly dissolves. Brush frequently over the lamb during the last 30 minutes of roasting.

Mint Glaze for Lamb

½ cup chopped fresh mint leaves   1 cup apple cider vinegar

In a small saucepan, combine the mint leaves and vinegar and cook over medium heat for 3 to 4 minutes until the vinegar is hot but not boiling. Remove from the heat and let the mixture steep for about 30 minutes. Use to baste lamb frequently during roasting.

Pineapple Glaze for Lamb

7 to 8 slices fresh or canned
   pineapple

About 1 hour before the end of roasting, cover the lamb with pineapple slices. Continue roasting until the meat is done and the pineapple is soft and browned and its natural juices glaze the meat.

Tomato Glaze for Lamb

½ cup ketchup   2 tablespoons Worcestershire sauce

In a small saucepan, combine the ketchup and Worcestershire sauce and heat over medium heat until the mixture is hot. Cool to tepid and use to baste lamb frequently during roasting.

Bar-B-Q Cocktail Sauce

(thanks to Clay King)

Makes about 2 cups

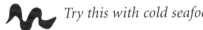 *Try this with cold seafood or use it as a veggie dip.*

2 cups Mild Bar-B-Q Sauce (page 155) or W'ham Mild Sauce

¼ cup prepared horseradish

1½ teaspoons Worcestershire sauce

Juice of 1 lemon

⅛ teaspoon garlic salt

⅛ teaspoon freshly ground black pepper

In a small saucepan, combine all the ingredients. Bring to a simmer over medium heat and cook, stirring occasionally, for about 30 minutes. Cool to room temperature.

Transfer to a glass container with a tightly fitting lid and refrigerate until ready to use. The sauce keeps for up to 1 week.

Horseradish Cocktail Sauce

(pure Willingham)

Makes about 1⅓ cups

 What's this good for? How about cold shrimp or crabmeat? Yum!

1 cup ketchup	A few drops of Tabasco sauce
¼ cup chili sauce	¼ teaspoon salt
1 tablespoon prepared horseradish	Freshly ground black pepper to taste
1 tablespoon freshly squeezed lemon juice	

In a glass or ceramic bowl, combine the ketchup, chili sauce, horseradish, lemon juice, Tabasco, and salt. Mix well and season with pepper. Serve immediately or chill until ready to use.

Tartar Sauce

(pure Willingham)

Makes ¾ cup

 With fish, of course! Fried, broiled, poached, grilled.

2	teaspoons chopped sweet pickle	¾	cup Mayonnaise (page 146) or
1½	teaspoons minced capers		store-bought mayonnaise
1	teaspoon minced onion	1	teaspoon minced parsley
1	teaspoon chopped green olives	1	teaspoon tarragon vinegar

Fold the pickle, capers, onion, and olives into the mayonnaise. Add the parsley and stir gently. Add the vinegar and stir to mix. Serve immediately or cover and refrigerate for up to 2 hours.

> You can change without growing
>
> But you can't grow without changing.

Chowchow

(anonymous)

Makes about 2 cups

This recipe was given to me by a customer who visited our restaurant in Collierville, Tennessee, in 1984. Unfortunately, I didn't get his name! I suggest you try it next time you have hamburgers or hot dogs. If you're feeding a crowd, double the recipe. The chowchow is also delicious on other sandwiches. Try it on roast beef, cheese, turkey—even barbecued pork! Wow.

½ cup yellow hot dog mustard
¼ cup ketchup
¼ cup Mild Bar-B-Q Sauce
    (page 155) or W'ham Mild Sauce

½ cup sweet relish, chilled
½ cup diced onions, chilled

In a saucepan, heat the mustard, ketchup, and barbecue sauce over medium-high heat, stirring, until simmering. Cook for 2 to 3 minutes to let the flavors blend. Remove from the heat and cool to room temperature.

Transfer to a glass or ceramic bowl, cover, and refrigerate until chilled. Just before serving, add the relish and onions. Mix well and serve immediately.

12

Desserts

Apple Pandowdy · John's Country Fruit Cobbler · Bee's Cobbler · Applescotch Crisp · Banana Cake with Chocolate Fudge Icing · Banana Split Dessert · Grandma's Raisin Bread Pudd'n with Rum Sauce · Southern Bread Pudding · Shoofly Pie · Old-Fashioned Custard Pie · Coffee Shop Oatmeal Cookies · Old-Time Oatmeal-Apple Cookies · Fudgy Frosted Brownies · White Chocolate Pecan Brownies · Key Lime Squares · Toffee Nut Bars · Butterscotch Sauce · Hot Fudge Sauce · Maple Sauce

 Who ever heard of a Southern social gathering without dessert? A barbecue is no different. After the last tasty morsel of tender barbecue is gone, the bowl of coleslaw is empty, and the corn bread is but a memory, there's only one thing to do. Serve dessert.

Down in this part of the world we like our desserts sinfully rich and sweet. No pussy-footin' around the notion of eating only "a little" or "just a bite." We enjoy dessert to the fullest. And the recipes in this chapter illustrate that philosophy.

There are recipes for wonderful fruit desserts, for luscious cakes and rich pies, giant cookies and decadent brownies. And then I share my best recipes for sweet sauces—which poured over anything don't just gild the lily—they make it so mucha bedda!

Apple Pandowdy

The question is, did the pandowdy derive its name from the term "dowdy" or did the Pennsylvania Dutch, whose recipe this is, invent the word "dowdy" to describe the dish? As far as I know, the term refers to someone who generally looks frumpy. This dessert is really quite pretty when it is first removed from the oven, but once the crust has been broken in several places, it takes on a decidedly dowdy appearance. Tastes great though! Scrumdelayosous.

Crust

1½ cups all-purpose flour
½ teaspoon salt

½ cup solid vegetable shortening, chilled
3 to 4 tablespoons cold water

Filling

1	teaspoon ground cinnamon	½	cup light molasses
¼	teaspoon ground nutmeg	2	tablespoons (¼ stick) butter
¼	teaspoon ground cloves		
¼	teaspoon salt		Whipped cream or vanilla ice cream,
9	medium apples, peeled, cored, and		for serving (optional)
	cut into ½-inch slices		

To make the crust, sift the flour and salt into a bowl. Add the shortening and, using 2 forks, a pastry blender, or your fingertips, toss until the mixture resembles coarse crumbs. Add enough water to hold the dough together. Gather it into a ball, wrap it with plastic wrap or waxed paper, and refrigerate for 1 hour.

Preheat the oven to 400°F. Grease 13 × 9 × 2-inch baking pan.

To make the filling, in a large bowl, combine the cinnamon, nutmeg, cloves, and salt. Add the apples and toss to coat. Transfer the apples to the baking pan. Drizzle the molasses over the apples. Dot with the butter.

On a lightly floured surface, roll out the chilled dough to a 13 × 9-inch rectangle. Beginning at one short end, fold the rectangle into thirds. Lay the folded dough on one end of the pan and gently unfold to cover the entire pan. Do not worry if the edges do not meet the sides of the pan.

Bake for 10 minutes. Reduce the oven temperature to 325°F and continue baking for about 30 minutes until the crust is golden and the filling is bubbling hot. Remove from the oven and push the crust into the apples in several places, so that the hot filling oozes up and over the crust. Cool for 20 minutes on a wire rack before serving warm with whipped cream or ice cream, if desired.

John's Country Fruit Cobbler

(thanks to John Teitsort)

Serves 8 to 10

A simple cobbler is the best darn way I know to end a great meal—and this one is a surefire winner. These old-fashioned, home-style fruit desserts are easier to make than pies, and used to be common daily fare in many farm kitchens. You can use any combination of fruit you like. This one relies on canned cherries or other fruit (which I happen to love), but fresh fruit is also delicious. Use what is in season.

Crust

3	cups all-purpose flour	1	cup solid vegetable shortening, chilled
1½	teaspoons salt		
			9 to 10 tablespoons ice water

Filling

2	16-ounce cans unsweetened cherries, apples, or blackberries	¼	cup cornstarch
¼	cup water	2	tablespoons (¼ stick) butter or margarine, melted and cooled, for brushing
¼	teaspoon vanilla extract		
2	cups sugar		

To make the crust, in a large bowl, combine the flour and salt. Add the shortening in pieces and using 2 forks, a pastry blender, or your fingertips, blend until the mixture resembles coarse crumbs. Add ice water until the dough holds together. Gather it into a ball, wrap it in waxed paper or plastic wrap, and refrigerate for at least 30 minutes, or until cold.

Preheat the oven to 350°F. Grease a 13 × 9 × 2-inch jelly roll pan.

On a lightly floured surface, roll half the dough out to a 15 × 12-inch rectangle. Return the other half to the refrigerator. Starting at one short end, fold the rectangle into thirds. Lay the folded package at one end of the pan and unfold, fitting it into the bottom and up the sides of the pan. Bake for about 5 minutes, or until barely crisp. Remove and cool on a wire rack.

To make the filling, in a large bowl, combine the fruit, water, and vanilla. In another bowl, whisk the sugar and cornstarch together and add to the fruit. Stir gently to mix well.

Pour the filling into the prepared pan and spread evenly.

On a lightly floured surface, roll the other half of dough out to a 12 × 8½-inch rectangle. Starting at one short end, fold the rectangle into thirds. Lay the folded package at one end of the pan and unfold gently over the filling. Carefully tuck the dough around the filling, leaving a little fruit showing.

Bake for 20 to 25 minutes, or until the filling is bubbling hot and the crust golden brown. Remove from the oven and brush with the melted butter. Cool slightly and serve.

Bee's Cobbler

(thanks to Mary Addis)

Serves 6

If all families could be as caring about their neighbors and loving of their own as are the Addises, what a grand world this would be. The Addises and the Willinghams shared a backyard fence when we lived in Little Rock, Arkansas, in the early 1960s, and in those days when I had to reach my wife, Marge, I called the Addises' house as readily as our own— certain I would find her there. Dessert was a must in the Addis household. Ice cream à la mode (!) was often served, as was this so-easy-to-make cobbler in which the fruit bakes submerged in the batter. Mary Addis says the cobbler is based on one that "Aunt Bee" prepared on The Andy Griffith Show, *and is known to many Arkansans, including the Clantons and McCoys of Hot Springs. You can use drained canned fruit instead of fresh fruit if you prefer.*

8	tablespoons (1 stick) margarine		Pinch of salt
1	cup all-purpose flour	1	cup milk
1	cup sugar	4	cups slightly sweetened sliced
2	teaspoons baking powder		peaches or fresh blackberries

Preheat the oven to 350°F. In a deep 10 × 8-inch (or 8 × 8-inch) baking dish, melt the margarine in the preheated oven.

In a bowl, whisk together the flour, sugar, baking powder, and salt. Stir in the milk and pour the batter into the baking dish.

Distribute the peaches over the batter. Bake for about 45 minutes, or until the batter rises over the fruit and is lightly browned and firm. Serve warm.

Note: *For a quick version, substitute 1 cup biscuit mix for the flour, baking powder, and salt.*

Applescotch Crisp

(pure Willingham)

Serves 12

 Whether you prefer the taste of butterscotch or vanilla, this crisp is a keeper—and so easy to make.

Filling

2 cups peeled and sliced tart apples (about 4 apples)

1 tablespoon all-purpose flour

½ cup firmly packed light brown sugar

½ cup water

¼ cup milk

Topping

⅔ cup all-purpose flour

½ cup quick-cooking rolled oats

½ cup chopped pecans or walnuts

8 tablespoons (1 stick) butter or margarine, melted

¼ cup sugar

1 teaspoon ground cinnamon

½ teaspoon salt

1 0.9-ounce package butterscotch or vanilla pudding mix (not instant)

Preheat the oven to 350°F.

To make the filling, in a large bowl, toss the apples with the flour, brown sugar, water, and milk. Mix well. Transfer to an ungreased 9-inch square baking pan.

To make the topping, in a bowl, combine the flour, oats, pecans, butter, sugar, cinnamon, salt, and pudding mix. Mix until crumbly. Sprinkle over the apples.

Bake for 45 to 50 minutes, or until the apples are tender and the topping is golden brown.

Banana Cake with Chocolate Fudge Icing

(thanks to Jo Grisham)

Serves 8 to 10

 Banana cake frosted with this old-fashioned fudge icing is just plain heavenly. Who can disagree with the flavor combination of bananas and chocolate?

Cake

1¼ cups sugar

½ cup solid vegetable shortening

2 large eggs

1 teaspoon baking soda

¼ cup buttermilk

1½ cups all-purpose flour

1 cup mashed bananas (about 3 bananas)

1 teaspoon vanilla extract

Icing

2 cups sugar

2 teaspoons unsweetened cocoa powder

8 tablespoons (1 stick) unsalted margarine

1 5.33-ounce can evaporated milk

1 teaspoon vanilla extract

To make the cake, preheat the oven to 350°F. Grease and flour two 8-inch round cake pans.

Using an electric mixer set on medium-high, cream the sugar and vegetable shortening until fluffy. Add the eggs, one at a time, mixing after each addition. In a small bowl, stir the baking soda into the buttermilk.

Add the flour to the batter, alternating it with the buttermilk. Mix well after each addition. Stir in the bananas and vanilla. Scrape the batter into the cake pans and bake in the center of the oven for 25 to 30 minutes, or until the edges pull away from the sides of the pan, the crust is golden brown, and a toothpick inserted near the center comes out clean. Invert onto wire racks to cool.

To make the icing, in a saucepan, combine the sugar, cocoa, margarine, and evaporated milk. Cook over medium-low heat, stirring, until smooth and the mixture forms a soft ball in the pan.

Remove from the heat and add the vanilla. Beat vigorously until the vanilla is incorporated and the icing is a smooth, spreadable consistency.

Spread about a third of the icing between the cooled layers. Use the remaining icing to frost the top and sides of the cake. Serve immediately or store under a cake dome or covered until ready to serve.

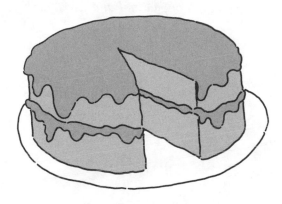

Use a cookie cutter to help decorate your cake by pressing the cutter lightly on the frosting and then tracing the outline with tinted icing from a pastry tube.

Banana Split Dessert

(thanks to Karen Yock Bigalk)

Serves 16 to 20

This is a dessert that is great for a party. It goes a long way, everybody loves it, and you make it hours ahead of time. Be sure you have room in your freezer before you begin— or you will find yourself shuffling the frozen peas and orange juice cans out of the way to make room for the fairly large jelly roll pan full of bananas and ice cream!

Crust

20 whole graham crackers

6 tablespoons (¾ stick) unsalted margarine, melted

Filling

3 to 4 bananas

½ gallon Neapolitan or strawberry ice cream (see the Note)

1 cup chopped walnuts

1 cup chocolate chips

8 tablespoons (1 stick) margarine

2 cups confectioners' sugar

1½ cups evaporated milk

1 teaspoon vanilla extract

1 pint heavy cream or frozen whipped topping

2 to 3 teaspoons sugar, or more to taste

To make the crust, in a food processor fitted with the metal blade, pulse the graham crackers to make crumbs. Alternatively, put the graham crackers in a large sealable plastic bag and crush them to crumbs by rolling a rolling pin over the bag.

Transfer the crumbs to a large bowl (reserve 2 to 3 tablespoons of dry crumbs for later use) and add the margarine. Using your fingers or a spoon, mix until blended. Spread the mixture over the bottom of a 15 × 11-inch jelly roll pan.

To make the filling, slice the bananas and arrange them in a single layer over the crust. Cut the ice cream into rounds about ¾ inch thick and lay them on top of the bananas. Sprinkle with the walnuts and freeze for at least 2 hours, or until firm.

In a saucepan, melt the chocolate chips and margarine over medium heat, stirring. Add the sugar and milk and cook, stirring, for about 5 minutes until thick and smooth. Remove from the heat and stir in the vanilla. Set aside to cool to warm room temperature. The mixture must maintain a pouring consistency.

Pour the cooled chocolate mixture over the banana–ice cream pie, spreading it to an even layer. Return the pie to the freezer for at least 2 more hours, or until firm.

Using an electric mixer set on medium-high, whip the cream until thick. Add the sugar and taste. Add more sugar if you like sweeter whipped cream. Whip the cream to soft peaks. Spread the whipped cream over the dessert. Sprinkle with the reserved graham cracker crumbs and freeze for another hour, or until firm.

Note: *Buy the ice cream in cylindrical containers. Let them warm up for a few minutes and then slide the whole cylinder out to make slicing the ice cream possible.*

Grandma's Raisin Bread Pudd'n with Rum Sauce

(thanks to Grandma Willingham)

Serves 8 to 10

Get ready for some down-home go-a-beggin' goodness, just like my grandpa enjoyed just about every Sunday!

Pudding

11 to 12 cups loosely packed day-old bread cubes (from a 12- to 18-slice loaf)

½ cup raisins

1 quart (4 cups) milk

¾ cup sugar

2 teaspoons ground cinnamon

1 teaspoon vanilla extract

¼ teaspoon salt

Sauce

1 cup evaporated milk

1 cup sugar

4 tablespoons (½ stick) butter

3 tablespoons cornstarch

¼ cup bourbon or rum or amaretto

To make the pudding, preheat the oven to 350°F. Grease a 13 × 9 × 2½-inch pan or roasting pan. Spread the bread cubes in the pan and toast for about 5 minutes, stirring at least once, or until lightly browned. Set aside.

In a small bowl, combine the raisins with enough hot water to cover. Soak for about 30 minutes.

In a saucepan, combine the milk, sugar, cinnamon, vanilla, and salt. Bring to a simmer over medium-high heat, stirring until smooth.

Drain the raisins and add to the saucepan. Stir to combine. Pour over the bread cubes, stir gently, and place in the oven. Reduce the oven temperature to 300°F and bake for about 45 minutes, or until the bread is soft, most the liquid is absorbed, and the custard looks set.

To make the sauce, in a saucepan, combine the evaporated milk, sugar, butter, and cornstarch. Bring to a simmer over medium-high heat, stirring until smooth. Remove from the heat and stir in the bourbon.

Spoon the pudding into dishes and top with the sauce.

If a recipe calls for confectioners' (powdered) sugar and you don't have any in the cupboard, make your own. Add one tablespoon of cornstarch to one cup of white, granulated sugar. Whir the mixture in the blender for about one minute until powdered.

Southern Bread Pudding

(thanks to Charlotte Helton Patterson)

Serves 8 to 10

Charlotte is one heck of a good cook. Try this bread pudding, a real down-home comfort food traditionally made with day-old bread and whatever spices are available. The sauce can be served as a plain vanilla sauce or spiked with a stronger flavor (see the Note).

Pudding

4 cups day-old bread cubes	3 large eggs, lightly beaten
8 tablespoons (1 stick) butter, melted	½ teaspoon ground nutmeg
1½ cups milk	⅛ teaspoon salt
1½ cups sugar	Ground cinnamon to taste
	½ cup raisins (optional)

Sauce

½ cup sugar	1 teaspoon light corn syrup
¼ cup buttermilk	¼ teaspoon baking soda
2 tablespoons (¼ stick) butter or margarine	½ teaspoon vanilla extract

To make the pudding, preheat the oven to 350°F. Grease a 2-quart casserole or baking dish. Put the bread cubes in the casserole and set aside.

In a bowl, combine the butter, milk, sugar, eggs, nutmeg, salt, and cinnamon. Whisk until well mixed and pour over the bread cubes. Fold in the raisins, if using. Bake for about 30 minutes, or until the pudding bubbles around the edges and looks partially set.

To make the sauce, in a saucepan, combine the sugar, buttermilk, butter, corn syrup, and baking soda and bring to a boil over high heat, stirring constantly. Continuing to stir, boil for 3 minutes. Remove from the heat and stir in the vanilla. Serve immediately, poured over the warm bread pudding.

Note: *To flavor the sauce, add freshly squeezed lemon juice, rum, or whiskey to taste after the sauce has boiled for 3 minutes and before adding the vanilla. Stir well and remove from the heat.*

Shoofly Pie

(pure Willingham)

Serves 6 to 8

Two of our desserts—this one and Apple Pandowdy (page 198)—bring back musical memories from the 1940s. Try this shoofly pie, which I adapted from an old Pennsylvania Dutch recipe, and make new memories!

1   store-bought 9-inch unbaked pie
    shell

Topping

1   cup all-purpose flour

½   cup lightly packed light brown
    sugar

¼   cup solid vegetable shortening,
    chilled

Filling

1   teaspoon baking soda

¼   teaspoon salt

1   cup boiling water

1   cup golden molasses

    Sweetened whipped cream or ice
        cream, for serving

Preheat the oven to 350°F. Bake the pie shell for about 5 minutes, or until barely crisp. Set on a wire rack to cool. Raise the oven temperature to 375°F.

To make the topping, whisk together the flour and sugar. Add the shortening in pieces and, using 2 forks, a pastry blender, or your fingers, blend until the mixture resembles coarse crumbs. Set aside.

To make the filling, in a large bowl, dissolve the baking soda and salt in the water. Add the molasses and stir until well mixed. Pour into the pie shell. Sprinkle the topping over the pie.

Bake in the center of the oven for 10 minutes. Reduce the oven temperature to 350°F and bake for about 30 minutes, or until the filling is set and does not jiggle when the pie is gently shaken. Do not overbake. Cool slightly on a wire rack. Serve warm with sweetened whipped cream or ice cream.

Note: *If you prefer, use your own favorite recipe for a homemade pie shell.*

Old-Fashioned Custard Pie

(thanks to Jo Grisham)

Serves 6 to 8

Nothing could be simpler than this simple Southern-style custard pie. No crust, no fuss. Just good eatin'. Smooth, soothing, not too sweet, not too rich—perfect after barbecue.

As do all pies, custard pies have a long culinary tradition in the South. Custard is made with ingredients available all the time in just about every kitchen: eggs, sugar, and milk or cream. One of the South's most famous custard pies is chess pie—which some claim got its name as a formalizing of the answer to the question "What kind of pie is this?" "Oh," the answer comes, "it's jes pie."

8	tablespoons (1 stick) unsalted margarine	4	large eggs, lightly beaten
1½	cups sugar	2	cups milk
½	cup self-rising flour	1	teaspoon vanilla extract
			Freshly grated nutmeg, for sprinkling

Preheat the oven to 300°F. Melt the margarine in a 9-inch pie plate in the oven.

In a bowl, combine the sugar, flour, eggs, milk, and vanilla. Pour into the pie plate. Sprinkle with nutmeg and bake for 45 to 50 minutes until the pie is just set around the edges but is still "shaky" in the center. Do not overbake. Cool on a wire rack before serving.

Coffee Shop Oatmeal Cookies

(thanks to Mrs. Larry Miller)

Makes about 5 dozen cookies

When Mrs. Miller shared this recipe with me, she explained that she learned how to make these chunky, chocolate chip–oatmeal cookies from her sister, who made them for the customers of the coffee shop where she worked. They are outstanding with coffee—in a coffee shop or in your own kitchen.

1 cup (2 sticks) unsalted margarine	1 teaspoon baking soda
1 cup packed dark or light brown sugar	2 teaspoons baking powder
½ cup granulated sugar	½ teaspoon ground cinnamon
2 large eggs	½ teaspoon salt
¼ cup milk or buttermilk	2 cups quick-cooking rolled oats
1 teaspoon vanilla extract	1 cup raisins (optional)
2 cups all-purpose flour	2 cups chocolate chips
	1 cup chopped pecans or walnuts

Preheat the oven to 350°F. Grease 2 baking sheets.

Using an electric mixer set on medium-high, cream the margarine and sugars until fluffy. Add the eggs, one at a time, mixing after each addition. Stir in the milk and vanilla and mix until smooth.

In another bowl, whisk together the flour, baking soda, baking powder, cinnamon, and salt. Add the dry ingredients to the creamed mixture in three batches, mixing until combined after each addition. Stir in the oats. Add the raisins, if using, chocolate chips, and pecans. Stir until well mixed.

Drop by teaspoonfuls onto the baking sheets, leaving about 2 inches between each cookie. Bake for 10 to 12 minutes, or until the edges are lightly brown and the cookies are golden brown. Cool on the baking sheets for 2 to 3 minutes and then transfer to wire racks to cool completely. Repeat until all the dough is used.

Old-Time Oatmeal-Apple Cookies

(pure Willingham)

Makes about 5 dozen cookies

Talk about chunky cookies! These are the very best—chock-full of raisins, walnuts, and apples. What texture! What flavor!

¾ cup butter-flavored solid vegetable shortening

1¼ cups packed dark brown sugar

1 large egg

¼ cup milk

1½ teaspoons vanilla extract

3 cups quick-cooking rolled oats

1 cup all-purpose flour

½ teaspoon baking soda

1¼ teaspoons ground cinnamon

¼ teaspoon ground nutmeg

½ teaspoon salt

1 cup diced apples

¾ cup raisins

¾ cup chopped walnuts

Preheat the oven to 375°F. Grease 2 baking sheets.

Using an electric mixer set on medium-high, cream the shortening and brown sugar until fluffy. Add the egg, milk, and vanilla and mix until smooth.

In another bowl, whisk together the oats, flour, baking soda, cinnamon, nutmeg, and salt. Stir the dry ingredients into the creamed mixture in three batches, mixing until combined after each addition.

Add the apples, raisins, and walnuts and stir until well mixed.

Drop by teaspoonfuls onto the baking sheets, leaving about 2 inches between each cookie. Bake for 12 to 13 minutes, or until the edges are lightly brown and the cookies are golden brown. Cool on the baking sheets for 2 to 3 minutes and then transfer to wire racks to cool completely. Repeat until all the dough is used.

Fudgy Frosted Brownies

(thanks to Hedwig Yock)

Serves 12 to 15

Brownies are an American favorite and are just right after a big outdoor meal. These, from my mother-in law, are among the fudgiest, most yummy I have ever popped in my mouth. And that's saying something!

Brownies

8 tablespoons (1 stick) lightly salted butter

2 ounces (2 squares) unsweetened chocolate, coarsely chopped

2 large eggs, lightly beaten

1 cup sugar

1 teaspoon vanilla extract

1 cup all-purpose flour

¼ cup milk

½ cup chopped walnuts

Frosting

2 tablespoons (¼ stick) lightly salted butter

1 ounce (1 square) unsweetened chocolate, coarsely chopped

2 cups confectioners' sugar, sifted

1 teaspoon vanilla extract

2 to 3 tablespoons heavy cream, if needed

To make the brownies, preheat the oven to 325°F. Grease a 15 × 11-inch jelly roll pan.

In a saucepan, melt the butter and chocolate, stirring, over medium-low heat. Transfer to a bowl.

Add the eggs and sugar and, using a wooden spoon, blend until smooth and even-colored. Add the vanilla and mix. Add the flour, alternating with the milk, beating after each addition until just mixed. Set aside to cool completely.

Fold the walnuts into the batter. Scrape into the pan, smooth the top, and bake for 15 to 20 minutes until a toothpick inserted near the center comes out slightly moist. Set the pan on a wire rack to cool.

To make the frosting, in a saucepan, melt the butter and chocolate, stirring, over medium-low heat, until smooth. Remove from the heat and add the sifted sugar. Whisk until smooth. Stir in the vanilla. Add a little cream to thin it out if the frosting is not a spreadable consistency. Spread over the cooled brownies. Cut into squares for serving.

A piece of raw potato in the container with the baked goods will keep them moist.

White Chocolate Pecan Brownies

(thanks to Liz Sutton)

Serves 12 to 15

The white chocolate is an appealing addition to these fudgy brownies—sort of dresses them up for fancy occasions. The brownies will seem undercooked when you remove them from the oven, but as long as the toothpick comes out clean, consider them done. The worst thing you can do is overbake them. Let them cool before cutting them into squares— they firm up during cooling.

continued

24	ounces semisweet chocolate, coarsely chopped	8	large eggs
14	tablespoons (1½ sticks plus 2 tablespoons) butter	3	cups all-purpose flour
		3	teaspoons salt
1	cup water	24	ounces white chocolate, coarsely chopped
3	cups sugar	4½	cups chopped pecans

Preheat the oven to 350°F. Grease a 15 × 11-inch jelly roll pan.

In the top of a double boiler set over simmering water, combine the dark chocolate and butter. Stir until the chocolate melts and the mixture is smooth. Transfer to the mixing bowl of an electric mixer and add the water and sugar. With the mixer on medium speed, beat until smooth.

Add the eggs, one at a time, beating to incorporate after each addition.

In another bowl, whisk together the flour and salt. With the mixer on medium-low, add the flour mixture to the chocolate mixture, a little at a time, until the batter is mixed and no white streaks of flour show.

Fold in the white chocolate and pecans. Scrape the batter into the pan and smooth the top. Bake for about 30 minutes, or until a toothpick inserted in the center comes out clean. Be careful not to overbake. Set the pan on a wire rack to cool completely. Cut into squares for serving.

A pinch of baking soda mixed in with the confectioners' (powdered) sugar keeps frosting made with the sugar from hardening.

Key Lime Squares

(thanks to Kristi "W'ham" Goldsmith)

Makes 12 to 16 squares

 Tangy and sweet all at once. And so fresh-tasting. These are a natural after a big meal of barbecue and all the trimmings.

Crust

1 cup (2 sticks) butter or margarine	2 cups all-purpose flour
½ cup confectioners' sugar, plus more for sprinkling	Pinch of salt

Filling

4 large eggs	6 tablespoons all-purpose flour
2 cups sugar	Grated zest of 1 lime
6 tablespoons freshly squeczed lime juice	

Preheat the oven to 350°F. Grease a 12 × 9 × 2-inch baking pan.

To make the crust, in a bowl, combine the margarine, sugar, flour, and salt. Mix with 2 forks or a pastry blender until crumbly. Press into the greased pan. Bake for 15 to 20 minutes, or until firm. Cool on a wire rack.

To make the filling, in a bowl, whisk the eggs until frothy. Add the sugar, lime juice, and flour and whisk until combined. Stir in the zest. Spread the filling over the crust and bake for about 25 minutes, or until the crust is lightly browned and the filling is set. Sprinkle with confectioners' sugar. Cool on a wire rack. When it's cool, cut it into squares.

Toffee Nut Bars

(thanks to Karla "W'ham" Templeton)

Makes about 24 bars

 This has got to be one of my all-time favorite desserts or midnight snacks.

Bars

8 tablespoons (1 stick) butter, softened	½ cup packed dark brown sugar
	1 cup all-purpose flour, sifted

Topping

2 large eggs, lightly beaten	½ teaspoon salt
1 cup packed dark brown sugar	1 cup sweetened shredded coconut
1 teaspoon vanilla extract	1 cup sliced almonds or chopped
2 tablespoons all-purpose flour	pecans
1 teaspoon baking powder	

Preheat the oven to 350°F.

To make the bars, in a bowl, cream the butter and brown sugar until light and fluffy. Add the flour and stir until combined. Press into an ungreased 13 × 9-inch baking pan. Bake for about 10 minutes, or until firm. Set on a wire rack to cool until set. Do not turn off the oven.

To make the topping, in a bowl, combine the eggs, brown sugar, and vanilla. Whisk until frothy. Add the flour, baking powder, and salt and whisk until mixed. Stir in the coconut and almonds. Spread over the crust. Bake for 20 to 25 minutes, or until the topping is golden brown. Cool on a wire rack. When it's cool, cut it into bars.

Butterscotch Sauce

(thanks to Kara "W'ham" Rose)

Makes about 2½ cups

Great spooned on ice cream or plain cake. Or just licked off the spoon. This sauce is especially thick and creamy because it's made with beaten egg whites.

4	tablespoons (½ stick) butter, softened	2	large eggs, separated
1	cup packed dark brown sugar	½	cup heavy cream
			Pinch of salt

Using an electric mixer set on medium-high, cream the butter and sugar until fluffy.

In a bowl, whisk the egg yolks until thick. Slowly whisk the cream into the yolks. Add to the creamed butter and sugar and mix until smooth.

Transfer the mixture to the top of a double boiler and heat over gently simmering water, whisking, until thick and hot.

Using an electric mixer set on medium, beat the egg whites until frothy. Add the salt and beat only to incorporate. Pour the egg yolk mixture into the whites. Beat until the sauce is thick and forms stiff, but not dry, peaks. Serve immediately.

> Remember you are not the center of the universe.
>
> That job has already been taken.

Hot Fudge Sauce

(thanks to Kara "W'ham" Rose)

Makes about ¾ cup

Chocolate sauce is good on ice cream, cake, brownies, berries, cherries—I guess it's good on just about anything you can think of!

1 tablespoon butter	1 cup sugar
1 ounce (1 square) unsweetened chocolate, coarsely chopped	2 tablespoons light corn syrup
⅓ cup boiling water	½ teaspoon vanilla extract
	⅛ teaspoon salt

In a saucepan, melt the butter. Add the chocolate and cook over low heat, stirring, until the chocolate melts. Gradually add the boiling water, stirring constantly. Add the sugar and corn syrup and stir until dissolved. Raise the heat to medium and simmer for 5 minutes.

Remove the sauce from the heat and stir in the vanilla and salt. Serve immediately.

Maple Sauce

(thanks to Kara "W'ham" Rose)

Makes about 1½ cups

Try this over baked apples, or how about spooned over a serving of the Apple Pandowdy on page 198? It's a treat over maple walnut ice cream too!

½   cup sugar

¼   cup corn syrup

¾   cup heavy cream

3   tablespoons butter

½   cup pure maple syrup

In a heavy saucepan, combine the sugar, corn syrup, and cream and heat to boiling, stirring constantly. Cook over high heat until the mixture registers 234°F on a candy thermometer. This is the soft ball stage: A droplet will form a very soft ball when dropped into a glass of cold water.

Remove the sauce from the heat and add the butter and maple syrup. Stir until incorporated. Serve immediately or cool and serve chilled.

Taste Testers

Jimmy Arnold, Cordova, TN

Harvard Bardwell, Baton Rouge, LA

Jon Bigalk, Apple Valley, MN

Dr. Jim Bishop, Murphresboro, TN

Betty Bogart, Little Rock, AR

Patrick Muldoon Brown, Sacramento, CA

Debbie Butterick, Memphis, TN

Vicky Chapin, Memphis, TN

Robert V. Chapman, Stuart, FL

Anne Chuck, Vienna, VA

Don Cobb, Lafayette, LA

Ned Faller, Lafayette, LA

Edie Fisher, Atlanta, GA

L. J. Goldstock, Meredith, NH

Robert Greggory, Boston, MA

Zane Grey, Ashdown, AR

Gene Gustafson, Memphis, TN

Nancy and Bob Hamel, Boston, MA

Debbie Haseltine, Bartlett, TN

Claire Hayes, Clinton, MS

Jeanne Hill, Memphis, TN

Gary Jacobs, Cleveland, OH

Ginger Johnson, Portland, OR

Willie Kircher, Scottsdale, AZ

Betty Lane, Kuttawa, KY

Pat Lee, North Reading, MA

Harold McMurray, Florence, AL

Lola Mathis, Columbia, MO

Mike Nooner, Rosamond, CA

Ida Notowitz, Memphis, TN

Dorthy and Bill Ojala, Aurora, MN

Peter Pettit, Memphis, TN

Pat and Roger Prior, Dallas, TX

Jerry Ruden, Memphis, TN

Rex Ryan, Germantown, TN

Chris Schlesinger, Cambridge, MA

Lyn Singley, Salt Lake City, UT

Roger Smith, Muskegon, MI

Daly Thompson, Los Angeles, CA

Lieutenant Governor John Wilder,
    Nashville, TN

Judge Robert J. Yock, Washington, DC

Dr. William J. Yock, St. James, MN

Max Younger, Cordova, TN

John Willingham's Major Awards

***

1983   First Place Ribs   *Memphis in May, Memphis, TN*

1983   Grand Champion   *Memphis in May, Memphis, TN*

***

1984   First Place Ribs   *Memphis in May, Memphis, TN*

1984   Grand Champion   *Memphis in May, Memphis, TN*

1984   First Place Beef   *American Royal, Kansas City, MO*

1984   First Place Pork   *American Royal, Kansas City, MO*

1984   First Place Lamb   *American Royal, Kansas City, MO*

1984   Grand Champion   *American Royal, Kansas City, MO*

***

1986   First Place Brisket   *South Fork Ranch BBQ, Dallas, TX*

1986   First Place Poultry   *South Fork Ranch BBQ, Dallas, TX*

1986   First Place Ribs   *South Fork Ranch BBQ, Dallas, TX*

1986   Gold Buckle Award Champion   *South Fork Ranch BBQ, Dallas, TX*

***

1987   First Place Spare Ribs   *World's Best Ribs, Richmond, VA*

1987   Grand Champion Ribs   *World's Best Ribs, Richmond, VA*

***

1989   First Place Pork Ribs   *Iowa State Fair BBQ, Des Moines, IA*

1989   First Place Beef Tenders   *Iowa State Fair BBQ, Des Moines, IA*

1989   First Place Ribs *Mississippi Valley BBQ Festival, Davenport, IA*

1989   First Place Beef/Tender *Mississippi Valley BBQ Festival, Davenport, IA*

1989   THE HICKORY SWITCH AWARD Best "Que" in *Memphis, Memphis, TN*

1989   First Place Lamb *American Royal Invitational, Kansas City, MO*

∿

1990   First Place Whole Hog *Memphis in May Invitational, Memphis, TN*

1990   First Place Beef Brisket *American Royal Invitational, Kansas City, MO*

1990   First Place Pork Shoulder *American Royal Invitational, Kansas City, MO*

1990   First Place Chicken Wings *American Royal Invitational, Kansas City, MO*

1990   First Place Spare Ribs *National Rib Cook-Off, Cleveland, OH*

1990   Grand Champion $25,000 *National Rib Cook-Off, Cleveland, OH*

∿

1991   First Place Whole Hog *Arkansas State Championship, Blythville, AR*

1991   First Place Whole Hog *Covington Jaycee BBQ, Covington, TN*

1991   First Place Ribs *Covington Jaycee BBQ, Covington, TN*

1991   First Place Whole Hog *City Fest 91, Tuscaloosa, AL*

1991   First Place Shoulder *City Fest 91, Tuscaloosa, AL*

1991   First Place Whole Hog *Christmas on the River, Demopolis, AL*

1991   First Place Ribs *Christmas on the River, Demopolis, AL*

1991   Grand Champion *Christmas on the River, Demopolis, AL*

1991   First Place Beef Brisket *Pine Castle BBQ Festival, Orlando, FL*

1991   First Place Whole Hog *Pine Castle BBQ Festival, Orlando, FL*

1991   First Place Shoulder *Pine Castle BBQ Festival, Orlando, FL*

1991   First Place Pork Shoulder *American Royal Invitational, Kansas City, MO*

1991   First Place Beef Brisket *American Royal Invitational, Kansas City, MO*

1991   Grand Champion *American Royal Invitational, Kansas City, MO*

1991   First Place Spare Ribs *National Rib Cook-Off, Cleveland, OH*

1991   Grand Champion $25,000 *National Rib Cook-Off, Cleveland, OH*

1991/1992 MEMPHIS IN MAY
SANCTIONED TOUR-COOKING
TEAM OF THE YEAR

~

1992 First Place Ribs *St. Jude/VFW BBQ
Festival, White Haven, MS*

1992 First Place Anything but Pork
Memphis in May, Memphis, TN

1992 First Place "Skinners Pasta"
Memphis in May, Memphis, TN

1992 First Place Ribs *Star Tribune's
Peoples Choice, Minneapolis, MN*

1992 Grand Champion *Star Tribune's
Peoples Choice, Minneapolis, MN*

1992 First Place Ribs Peoples Choice
BBQ Festival, Norfolk, VA

1992 First Place Sauce Peoples Choice
BBQ Festival, Norfolk, VA

1992 Grand Champion Peoples Choice
BBQ Festival, Norfolk, VA

1992 First Place Lamb *American Royal
Invitational, Kansas City, MO*

1992 First Place Brisket *American Royal
Invitational, Kansas City, MO*

1992 BEST SAUCE ON THE PLANET
*American Royal Invitational, Kansas
City, MO*

1992 Grand Champion Reserve
*American Royal Invitational, Kansas
City, MO*

1992 First Place Poultry *Great Yankee
BBQ, Boston, MA*

1992 First Place Pork Shoulder *Great
Yankee BBQ, Boston, MA*

1992 First Place Ribs Peoples Choice
Great Yankee BBQ, Boston, MA

1992 Grand Champion Peoples Choice
Great Yankee BBQ, Boston, MA

~

1993 Grand Champion Chicken
*American Pitmasters BBQ Group,
Boston, MA*

1993 First Place "Hot Stuff" Rub
*American Royal Invitational, Kansas
City, MO*

1993 First Place Pork *Jumer's Casino
BBQ, Rock Island, IL*

1993 First Place Brisket *Jumer's Casino
BBQ, Rock Island, IL*

1993 First Place Pork *American Royal
Invitational, Kansas City, MO*

1993 First Place Brisket *American Royal
Invitational, Kansas City, MO*

1993 First Place Ribs *Pig and Pepper
Championship, Carlisle, MA*

1993 First Place Pork *Pig and Pepper
Championship, Carlisle, MA*

1993 BEST COOKER IN THE WORLD
Memphis in May, Memphis, TN

~

1994   First Place Brisket   *Massachusetts State Championship, Lexington, MA*

1994   First Place Chicken   *Massachusetts State Championship, Lexington, MA*

1994   Peoples Choice Ribs   *Massachusetts State Championship, Lexington, MA*

1994   Grand Champion   *Massachusetts State Championship, Lexington, MA*

1994   First Place Shoulder   *Blue Ridge BBQ Championship, Tryon, NC*

1994   Grand Champion Reserve   *Blue Ridge BBQ Championship, Tryon, NC*

1994   First Place Beef Brisket   *American Royal Invitational, Kansas City, MO*

1994   First Place Farmland Ribs   *American Royal Invitational, Kansas City, MO*

1994   Grand Champion Farmland   *American Royal Invitational, Kansas City, MO*

∿

1995   First Place Hot Sauce   *American Royal Invitational, Kansas City, MO*

1995   First Place Mild Vinegar Sauce   *American Royal Invitational, Kansas City, MO*

1995   First Place Cajun Hot Sauce   *American Royal Invitational, Kansas City, MO*

1995   The Quinn Award for Barbecue Excellence   *Jonesboro, AR*

1995   First Place Beef/Seafood Pasta Anything but Pork   *Southern Spring Fest, Southhaven, MS*

1995   Grand Champion Anything but Pork   *Southern Spring Fest, Southhaven, MS*

No Brag Just Fact

To Order Willingham's World Champion Seasonnings,

Sauces, Spices, Mustard, Rubs, and Marinades

phone or fax

1-800-737-WHAM (9426)

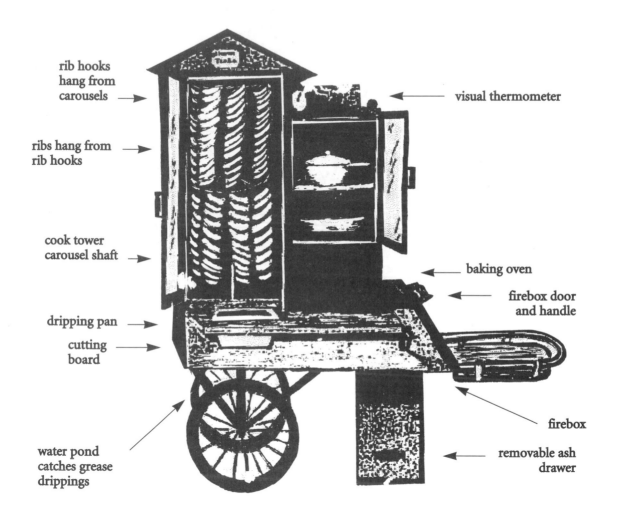

rib hooks
hang from
carousels

ribs hang from
rib hooks

cook tower
carousel shaft

dripping pan

cutting
board

water pond
catches grease
drippings

visual thermometer

baking oven

firebox door
and handle

firebox

removable ash
drawer

"W'HAM TURBO COOKER"
(WC-₁₂BYV₂₀)

Index